Media Relations

To Maria,

with thanks.

David Herle

10/05

Media Relations

✦

From a Journalist's Perspective

David Henderson

iUniverse, Inc.

New York Lincoln Shanghai

Media Relations
From a Journalist's Perspective

iUniverse books may be ordered through booksellers or by contacting:

iUniverse
2021 Pine Lake Road, Suite 100
Lincoln, NE 68512
www.iuniverse.com
1-800-Authors (1-800-288-4677)

ISBN: 0-595-34595-6

Printed in the United States of America

In loving memory of
Louise S. Henderson
1913–1983

Contents

MEDIA RELATIONS FIELD GUIDE

Introduction

I have never thought there was any magic about getting good media coverage for my clients.

A lady I knew at Hill & Knowlton Public Relations once told me that media relations was a science. It is not a science, either.

Effective media relations, the kind that delivers the results you desire, is not magic and it is not science—it is not even art; it is an imperfect craft, at best. But it can be powerful. It comes from knowing what makes a news story, finding a reporter who agrees with you and working with the reporter to develop a story you'll be pleased with.

When I made the career jump from network news correspondent at CBS News to running a public relations agency, it seemed only natural to me that effective media relations for my clients would begin with figuring out a news angle that would appeal to a particular reporter.

But what I learned over the intervening years is that few public relations people ever consider what a reporter needs for a story. Even fewer have ever bothered to develop working relationships with the news media, preferring instead to send news releases indiscriminately to as many journalists as possible. And fewer still have any experience actually working in the news business.

A few years back, while teaching a class in media relations at the University of Virginia, I faced a real challenge. I could find no university-level textbook on media relations that even had a hint of recognition of the needs of the news media. What I found were textbooks on writing news releases, as if we really need more releases flooding or "carpet bombing" the news media.

So this book is a first—a field guide on how to do effective media relations in a multimedia world, written from the perspective and experience of working journalists.

It provides anyone who works with the news media a wider understanding and perspective into how news functions, how a journalist or reporter judges the value of a story and what he or she needs to write one.

I asked a group of friends and colleagues in the news business to share their thoughts and tips—journalists from some of the top newspapers, wire services and broadcast news organizations in America, Canada and Britain.

The result is this working guide on media relations from the viewpoint of journalists. It is a look inside the news business and a resource to help you communicate clearly and accurately with reporters, editors and producers; control messages to the best possible extent; craft a story idea to make it sound appealing and easy to cover for a reporter; and achieve accurate, credible and effective coverage in the news media.

There are few greater thrills than opening a newspaper or turning on a newscast to see a favorable, balanced news story about your company, your organization or yourself. Accurate news coverage, with its implied third-party endorsement, is credible and considered to be far more influential than paid advertising.

Effective media relations doesn't work the way that most people think and certainly not the way that many PR people practice it. It's actually simpler and certainly more straightforward. It's also more powerful than any other component in an organization's marketing arsenal. First and foremost, it is *relationship-based*.

Whether used in building a brand, marketing a product or service or promoting an image, knowing how the media thinks about news and what they are looking for in a story will give you a significant competitive edge in helping to achieve your goals, whatever they might be.

David Henderson
Alexandria, Virginia

GETTING TO KNOW
THE NEWS MEDIA

Give the Media a Story

Welcome to life in a multimedia world, an environment that is constantly changing, taking new shape and then, reinventing itself all over again. A world in which, for journalists, every minute can be a deadline. A world where what you say in Chicago can be reported almost instantly in London, Singapore and everywhere in between via the Internet, wire services and satellite television news. A world where many things are competing for the media's attention. And a world where the news media you knew last year isn't the same news media you have to know today.

In today's highly competitive world, a good news story positions you as a leader, as someone special. Besides being a heady drug for your ego, having the media write about you builds reputations and enhances brands. It will help drive awareness and interest in your organization quicker than anything else. It opens doors to audiences that might otherwise remain out of reach. Media coverage can make and break legends. A good story in the media can right a wrong.

Yet for many individuals, businesses and organizations that want to reach wide audiences, effective media relations remains all too elusive. In the last couple of decades, since the value of media relations has been recognized as a powerful brand-building and marketing tool, corporations have spent millions on public relations efforts, trying to win favorable positioning in their respective marketplaces by using the awesome reach of the news media, the powerful conduit to the public. And still, many organizations feel shortchanged.

Part of the reason is that not many people who are assigned the task of dealing with journalists or even many so-called media relations experts have ever worked a day in a newsroom. Media relations can be done without such experience, of course, but someone with a background in the working news media generally knows how journalists think, what they are

3

looking for and what is needed, from the reporter's perspective, to make a *story*—as opposed to so much public relations fluff.

Sometimes, to get the media's attention, the story needs an unusual twist. In a tough competitive bid against a major entertainment publicity firm in Los Angeles, my agency won the account to launch the new image of a still relatively unknown place called Branson, Missouri. Branson is a place where many respected senior citizen stars of the country music world have settled to perform.

Andy Williams has his Moon River Theater. The Presley family (no relation to the "King of Rock 'n' Roll") have their Country Jubilee Theatre. Ray Stevens has his own theatre, and so does a popular country music violinist named Shoji Tabuchi. More than 30 luxurious music halls have been built in Branson in the last 15 years.

No one seems to know why this started or why so many country music performers were attracted to Branson, but the theatres are filled with fans every afternoon and evening, and the shows are terrific. Perhaps Branson is best chalked up as a middle-class American phenomenon.

When we began working with Branson, awareness of the town was limited to a few surrounding states. Attendance was an already fairly impressive 1.3 million a year. But local entertainment leaders had a bigger dream.

Theatre owners had formed an association, the Ozark Marketing Council, which was our client. They had two goals—boost national awareness for Branson and push up the annual number of visitors to 3.5 million within two years. They wanted to meet those goals solely through media relations.

Clearly, an entertainment publicity angle, focusing on the individual country music stars, could not achieve those goals. That approach, while fairly logical, just could not reach and excite the sheer number of people that Branson needed because it would be limited largely to the entertainment media.

Our plan was to capitalize on Branson's allure of being relatively "unknown." Something new and trendy. A little research showed that Branson had already eclipsed Nashville in annual visitors and was starting to get into the league of places like Disneyworld. So, we planned a "grand opening" of Branson's new season of stars, and the pitch to the national news media went something like this:

"Let me tell you about a place you have never heard of. It's called Branson, Missouri. It's in the Ozarks of southern Missouri and only reachable by two-lane mountain blacktop. But last year, Branson attracted nearly one-third the total number of tourists of Disneyworld. And yet, you have never heard of the place. Right?" We always stopped there to let those impressive nuggets of information sink in and get a reaction.

Then, we continued, "The tourists are there because nearly every country music star you can name—from Steamboat Willie to Willie Nelson to Mel Tillis—is performing at the dozens of music halls along that two-lane blacktop. And the biggest season ever starts in three weeks. Everybody will be there...." By the end of that pitch, we had their attention most of the time, and we got big results.

During that two-week grand opening at Branson, we attracted coverage and live broadcasts by The Today Show, CBS Morning News, *Time*, *People*, *Newsweek*, NBC Evening News, CBS Evening News, ABC Evening News, Associated Press, Reuters, the *New York Times*, The Larry King Show, Regis Philbin (then with Kathie Lee), countless local television news remotes from across the country, too many newspapers to count and, of all things, the *Wall Street Journal*, which wrote a glowing editorial about the Branson phenomenon.

Literally overnight, millions of people all across America learned about Branson, and all because of media relations.

Branson's star took off like, well, a shooting star. That season alone, the town attracted more than three million visitors. There were traffic jams for days on that now-famous two-lane blacktop. The theatres, theme parks, motels, curio shops and restaurants were packed. And it didn't let up for years. Branson, Missouri, became a world-famous entertainment mecca almost overnight, and it all began with a clever twist on a timely and trendy story for the news media.

Our approach in presenting the story to the media had focused not on the obvious, the dozens of country music stars performing at Branson, but on a phenomenon that appealed to the national news media. Here was an entertainment center that few decision-makers at the major media centers were aware of but was attracting millions of visitors.

Our strategy was to play to the natural curiosity of the people who decide what news organizations cover and report. Most of them are in New York and, at the time, most of those folks in New York had never heard of Branson. The phenomenon captured their attention, and the coverage was fantastic.

One of the easiest ways to achieve good media relations seems to be the hardest for public relations people to understand. People in the news business make their living writing stories that appear in newspapers, wire services, magazines and on television and radio. To do this, they need something new—a hook, an angle. Learn what they need for a news angle, give them a legitimate story, provide balanced background information and the news media will be happy. And you will have a good story to your credit.

All About Who You Know

Journalists don't give most people in public relations, with a few exceptions, high marks for knowing how to develop a legitimate news story, get the story before the news media and cultivate trusted relationships with reporters and editors.

For many public relations (PR) agencies, media relations efforts have remained stalled for too long by predictability, traditional tactics and simply not keeping pace. All too often, they come up short in the areas of authentic, trusted media relationships, journalistic skills and knowledge of what makes news.

And all too often, the key assignment of pitching stories to the news media is handed to the youngest members of a public relations agency or a communications department, with little or no training or preparation.

"Sometimes they sound as bored and rote as a telemarketer, and you know the PR agency has dispensed an intern to read off a sheet," says Linda Stasi of the *New York Post*. "Don't waste my precious daily deadline time like this. It's not fair to me, and it's not fair to the poor intern who probably gets the brunt of it all!"

In response to client concerns, improving media relations skills has been targeted as a top priority by several major public relations agencies in the United States and Britain. Clients have an ever-increasing need to reach audiences through the media in a timely way. Unquestionably, corporate clients of PR firms, constantly seeking a competitive edge, want strategic counsel and lofty ideas. But they also want the immediate payoff of effective media relations.

Clients expect public relations experts to have deep media connections and close working relationships with all the most powerful journalists, whether in times of crisis or for routine product promotion.

"Media relations," says Brian Lamb, founder and chief executive officer of C-SPAN, "is about relationships. A reporter needs to know who you are. It's as important as what you have to say. If you have a great announcement but have not established a contact or relationship in the media, no one will pay attention."

But it's hard for PR people to develop those relationships if they don't understand how people in the media operate.

"They are not sensitive enough to deadlines," says National Public Radio's Barbara Bradley Hagerty of the public relations people who contact her. "They don't bother to ask, to find out whether you are in the middle of something, they just launch into a pitch. Most public relations people don't know how journalists work. Most PR people are not quick enough in responding."

Richard Danbury, producer for Newsnight on BBC Television News, says "many public relations people (not all) are quite unsophisticated. Then again, I suppose many journalists are unsophisticated, too."

Danbury faults PR people for arrogance in their lack of sophistication, as he calls it, and being too lazy to research the media before pitching a story.

"I'm not impressed with the job PR people do," says Pat Piper, long-time broadcast producer and writer for Larry King. "If I say 'no thanks'—I get a bunch of crap about why I'm wrong and how the boss will be contacted."

The problem is usually simple—public relations people just have not invested the time to know how the media works, what the media needs in the way of a story idea, who to contact in the media or how to make a story pitch.

"PR people just don't do their homework," says Steve Scully, long-time producer at C-SPAN. "For example, don't call me about a segment on gardening, when C-SPAN does politics, issues, books and events."

Media relations remains a mystery for many executives and PR practitioners, a seemingly vague thing that often involves hiring an agency to do something intangible, that may or may have any results. It is common to hear company executives express their displeasure to their public relations people at spending vast sums of money on media relations campaigns that totally miss the mark.

Many journalists are fully aware that corporations often fumble and miss excellent opportunities to be heard and gain valuable publicity when their public relations people don't have the right connections and knowledge of the media.

Andrew Buncombe, Washington correspondent for London's *Independent* newspaper, says, "Sometimes I cannot believe the opportunities that big companies let pass when I am seeking a comment from them on a story that is at worst neutral and at best very much in their favor. Some [public relations people] are pathetic."

The most important thing, Buncombe says, "is to understand the market and understand the media outlet you are trying to pitch the story to. No media organization operates without a degree of bias in the stories they promote—the PR person needs to study that."

"Successful PR people have a 'service' attitude, as opposed to one based on 'spin control,'" comments long-time Washington, DC, newspaperman Lyle Denniston. "And successful people understand that 'service' means melding their assistance to the media with loyally serving their client. The two can go together."

But there is hope. Overall, in talking with journalists about the value of media relations to their work in the news business, I found a healthy attitude. Journalists do need people who will give them good stories on a regular basis. They are open to ideas. And they believe that communications people can make a significant contribution to both helping their clients or employers build favorable awareness while providing valuable assistance to the media.

As Scott Simon, the popular host of Weekend Edition on National Public Radio, said, "You [PR people] are part of an honorable profession. The sanctimony of so many of us journalists aside—I think there is probably about the same proportion of scoundrels to saints in both lines. Cheerfulness counts for a lot."

The first tenet of effective media relations is to passionately embrace the reality that it's a relationship-driven discipline. It really is about who you know in the news media and the level of trust you have developed.

The people assigned to the job of media relations need reporters and reporters need the stories and resources they have to offer. But it doesn't begin as a two-way street. It begins with outreach. The challenge in media relations is to find the right journalists and earn their trust, through understanding of their needs, factual information and a healthy measure of good humor.

It's the "News Media"!

At first blush, you may think this is not a big deal or just nit-picking terminology. You may be right. Then again, perhaps not.

The difference between "press" and "media" is subtle but important. Understanding the difference is important if you are to be effective in media relations. At the very least, it shows you are savvy about the news media.

The term "press" originated from the printing press and has been associated with the newspaper business for decades. A caricature of the press evolved in black and white motion pictures years ago of reporters with large "press cards" stuck in the brims of their hats, sometimes lugging big cameras that fired off golf ball-sized "flash bulbs." Those days are over and gone.

Nonetheless, hundreds of Web sites for organizations large and small still refer visitors to their "press room." Such use of the word screams at site visitors that this is an organization that is…well, not keeping up with the times.

To many journalists, knowing the difference between "press" and "media" quietly says something about you and your level of knowledge and awareness in media relations. I've known some broadcast reporters who are offended when someone called them the "press." They are not, so why call them that? It may not be a deal breaker, as to whether they do a story or not but it's the sort of thing that can get you off on the wrong foot with a reporter. You never know how a broadcast news person or any journalist thinks about being called "press." Play it safe and professional.

In this era of 24-hour cable news programs, up to the minute Internet news services and rapidly changing methods of instantly reporting the news from virtually anywhere on earth, the term "press" is passé and about as old-fashioned as an old typewriter.

"News media" or simply, the "media," refers to the organizations and the people who cover, report, edit, direct and produce the news, from television and radio to newspapers, magazines and the Internet.

Today's journalists are members of the "news media," not the press.

Journalism Driven by Profits

To understand effective media relations is to understand the news business. The way in which the business called "journalism" is practiced today has changed at almost light speed in recent years. Once focused on reporting events of interest and happenings that might affect our lives, the focus of news now is on how to make the greatest profit.

Years ago, I walked into the main newsroom of CBS Network News in New York as a very naïve young man from northern Virginia and began working alongside some of the icons of broadcast news—Walter Cronkite, Douglas Edwards, Richard C. Hottelet, Dan Rather, Mike Wallace, Dallas Townsend, Morley Safer. I had always wanted to be a broadcast journalist, and here I was among some of the best. It was one of the most exciting times in my life.

No one back then thought of CBS News as a profit center. The purpose of CBS News and the other networks was to credibly report the news of the day without being encumbered by an eye on ratings and corporate stock value.

At that time CBS News had a full staff of seasoned editors and producers who checked the facts and looked over every script before it went on the air. That's the way it was at many of the networks and major papers. The emphasis was on quality and solid journalism. We were expected to report the news. It's not that way today.

Over the last 20 years, many once-respected news operations have dramatically cut back on news staffs, and quality has suffered.

Once an altruistic and perhaps too idealistic profession with keen focus on balance, accuracy and integrity, journalism is today driven by corporate profits...money. Big media conglomerates discovered in the 1980s that news, like entertainment, can be a money machine. The higher their ratings in radio and television news, the more they can demand from advertisers. The bigger the headlines in print, the bigger the flow of ad dollars.

Consequently, news today is presented less to inform and more to titillate, seduce and entertain. All this has happened at a time when news audiences are being pulled away from traditional news outlets by cable television and Internet news sources.

"We're in a period of change and dislocation," said Tom Rosenstiel, of Columbia University's Graduate School of Journalism. "Clearly, some of the older media are suffering."

Trust in news sources is down drastically, according to "The State of the News Media 2004" by the Project for Excellence in Journalism, a project Rosenstiel headed at Columbia University, funded by the Pew Charitable Trusts.

According to the Columbia study, the percentage of people who believe what they read in newspapers has declined from 80 percent in 1985 to 59 percent in 2003, and the percentage who give high grades for credibility to the network news divisions dropped from 74 percent in 1996 to 65 percent in 2002.

In television, the study found a declining amount of airtime devoted to actual news, as opposed to other content like commercials and promotions. Taken together, the nightly network newscasts, which run for 30 minutes, average 18 minutes and 48 seconds of news, down 11 percent from 1991. On network morning shows, the average is 15 minutes and six seconds of news per half-hour.

The study found that English-language newspaper circulation has declined 11 percent since 1990, while network evening newscast ratings are down 34 percent over the last decade.

In general, the study found, corporate profits have increased or held steady while investments in newsgathering have declined. Today, newspapers employ 2,200 fewer people than they did in 1990. Between 1991 and 2000, newspaper profits increased 207 percent, the study found, but newsroom jobs increased just three percent.

A similar trend is clear in television. The number of correspondents employed by the evening newscasts is down more than 33 percent since 1985, and the number of overseas bureaus has been cut in half.

In cable news, again according to the Columbia study, 62 percent of the air time consists of live broadcasts, which are often cheaper than prepared, packaged reports. And the vast majority of stories reported on cable consist of a few "big stories" of the day.

In one 16-hour broadcast day, the study found, only 27 percent of stories were new reports that hadn't been mentioned earlier. Fully 68 percent of stories were segments that repeated the same information over and over again, without any new reporting.

The result, the study said, is a "jumbled, chaotic, partial quality in some reports, without much synthesis...of the information." As the satirist Jon Stewart has observed, some of television news has turned into a "nonsensical gong show."

It is in this environment that the modern media relations professional works. It's more challenging and more competitive than ever before to get the media's attention and achieve accurate coverage—requiring a savvy understanding of news media trends.

While it used to be that all we needed to do was give a reporter an idea for a story, today we must be prepared to provide a lot more, including anything that will help a reporter convince his or her editor that the story is worthwhile and relevant.

Media relations today requires us to nurture the story development process along once we've found interest from the media. We have to provide all kinds of background information, details and guidance to a journalist, while always keeping the focus on how we would like the story to come out. It's often time-consuming, but the payoff is big when you land great coverage.

Is media relations worth all the effort? You bet! The news media, despite a sometimes rocky and profit-driven evolution over the last couple of decades, remains the most powerful form of communication in America, second only to swapping gossip over the office water cooler.

The Ratings Game

Effective media relations in today's world mandates that communicators—including public relations people—work harder than ever to understand how stories occur and how news happens. Communications people also need to try, whenever possible, to stay ahead of trends in news coverage.

Public relations people need "a reality check," says Linda Ellerbee, a television reporter, anchor and producer with three decades of distinguished work. "We are in the middle of a seismic shift in how we, and the rest of the world, receive our news," she says.

Today's news in general, and television news in particular, is more focused on immediacy than accuracy, Ellerbee says.

Neal Shapiro, executive producer of NBC Dateline for several years, agrees. He told me that television news is solely about "ratings, ratings, ratings." That's how his program decides what stories to air. Whatever story will attract the biggest audience is the story that television news will report. Gone are the days when the purpose was purely to inform. Instead, the quest for ratings directly drives editorial content.

Consider stories coming out of small communities that have taken on worldwide importance, such as the Laci Peterson case—a tragic local story that included murder, adultery, betrayal and pregnancy. Although without any real international relevance, the case became international news for months, at times capturing headlines ahead of terrorism and wars.

In order to capture attention for our news and to tell our story, we face stiff competition. There are new challenges at every turn. Someone or some event of the day is always out there with a sexier angle or more timely approach.

To stay ahead of this game, you need to know the players. "My one piece of advice for people in the PR industry," says Lisa Guernsey of the

New York Times, "would be to get to know the reporters to whom you are pitching. Know their beats. Know their most recent stories. Know the personalities of the sections that they write for."

Linda Ellerbee offers eight tips for public relations people looking to get savvier when working with the media:

1. Remember that a public relations professional's job is to change things. A reporter's job is not.

2. If you are simply trying to raise publicity, buy an ad. Remember that reporters need to see the context of your message.

3. Just because you are worthy, it doesn't mean you are newsworthy. Find the story within the theme.

4. Know what reporters are looking for before you pitch them a story.

5. Make a media friend. They know what a good story looks like, and their input can be valuable.

6. Never lie to a reporter. It will ruin your reputation.

7. Don't contact a reporter with a full story unless they invite you to. Give them a simple, to-the-point summary on initial contact.

8. Remember that good reporters love good PR people. A healthy, professional relationship makes everyone's job easier.

At my marketing communications agency, I used to coach our younger team members about media relations by saying that they either needed to make friends and contacts in the news media or learn to accept rejection gracefully. People in media relations must stay open to new approaches and ideas. They need to be aware of the media's never-ending appetite for some new and different twist on a story, the current "flavor of the day." And they should never take it personally when they get turned down.

Getting your story before the news media can be done but it requires a level of smart planning and hard work to really understand how the news media operates and what its needs are. And it starts by understanding what reporters need for a story and then finding imaginative and timely news angles to get their attention.

Media relations today is a whole new ballgame, and you've got to keep up with the game in order to score points.

One Size Does Not Fit All

It wasn't that long ago that newspaper editors and broadcast news producers sat in ivory towers and ran stories that they believed their broad audiences would need to know about.

There's the legendary story, for example, that on the day that the Three Mile Island nuclear reactor nearly melted down in March 1979 in Pennsylvania, CBS Evening News chose to lead with a story about Britain's Queen Elizabeth because the producers in New York thought that, in the realm of world events, the Queen was more important. Today, nobody remembers the story about the Queen but a lot of people remember Three Mile Island.

Media decision makers today are keenly aware of who their primary audiences are and what kind of news is most likely to appeal to them. It's not only "All The News That's Fit To Print," as the *New York Times* says. It's also the news that you are likely to be interested in and talk about with your friends and colleagues. That's how popular newspapers and broadcast news programs become even more successful—by focusing on stories that appeal to audiences, journalism that sells newspapers and magazines and builds audiences for broadcast stations, networks and cable channels.

The kind of story, for example, that runs on the front page of one daily newspaper might not appeal to editors at another newspaper in the same city. For all kinds of reasons—political, cultural, economic, demographic, social—each media outlet has its own primary target audiences.

USA Today, for example, has a style geared to business people on the run, with incisively written and very timely stories encapsulated in as few words as possible. *USA Today* wants to make sure you learned about it first from them.

Its detractors have called *USA Today* the "McPaper" because, like fast food, you can consume it quickly and there is little nourishment or depth.

Some of the paper's features amount to little more than "nuggets" of information that editors believe their readers want. But, it's been highly successful for two decades because it knows and focuses on specific audiences.

USA Today has essentially reinvented the way news is presented, using crisp color, editorial content and visuals. The paper has forced other media decision-makers to rethink their broad marketing appeal and re-evaluate how they fit on the competitive landscape, in order to stay in business.

It's not surprising that the type of in-depth news analysis you find in the *New York Times* won't appear in *USA Today*. Both newspapers are popular and respected yet each has an entirely different approach to covering news. Each has its own primary audience. So, while any news organization—whether newspaper or broadcast or magazines—wants to capture the largest audience possible, they have carefully defined primary audiences, and they work hard to feel the pulse of those audiences.

Today's effective media relations professional must also have his or her finger on that "pulse," evaluate the journalistic trends and even the politics of several different news organizations in order to find the right "home" for a favorable story. A story that would be perfect for National Public Radio might be dismissed by the more conservative producers at Fox News.

Beyond the more traditional news media is today's 24-hour news cycle and the instant reach of Internet news sites and news-oriented blogs (Web journals). We live in the age of "instant" news coverage, when a story carried on the Associated Press wire in America can appear on the Web site of a newspaper in Melbourne, Australia, in the blink of an eye.

So, in media relations, how do you find the best place for your story?

- Target. Make a list of communities or cities or places where you want news of your organization to appear. Include trade magazines and think about whether your story might cross over and appeal to trades in more than one industry sector. Call it your "shopping list" because, as when we go to the mall, sometimes our shopping list is a little grander than our budget.

- Get smart about specific publications and news outlets on your shopping list. Have they covered your type of story before, what are their political influences or overtones, what are the general demographics of their audience and what sort of depth might they devote to a story about your organization? Believe it or not, the *National Inquirer* may be a terrific way to reach an enormous audience segment with a consumer-oriented story that might not appeal to editors at the *Los Angeles Times*.

• Shoot high. Just because the *Wall Street Journal* has never before reported on your industry sector doesn't mean they are not interested in your company. As head of corporate communications at Gulfstream Aerospace, I found that while most business reporters hadn't been interested for years in a stereotypical story pitch about the merits of business aircraft, they were attracted to a skillfully crafted story pitch about the hot trend among corporations of buying ultra-expensive, ultra-long-range business jets. When I invited select groups of top-level journalists from around the world to experience a flight aboard the $40-million Gulfstream V at 50,000 feet, far above all other aircraft traffic, and at a speed faster than most commercial airliners, it always guaranteed a great story. They always mentioned one of our key selling points—that the Gulfstream V is the world's longest range high performance business jet. The same story angle about the Gulfstream V appeared in every major publication and television news outlet around the world, and during that time, orders for the new aircraft increased 443 percent.

In today's style of media relations, part of the trick to capturing a reporter's attention is to begin by identifying the right media outlet for your story, with keen attention to online news sites.

Be Friendly, Be Funny and Be Honest

We are in a new era for both the news media and media relations people. And there are high hopes on both sides.

The news media has in recent years been faced with its own concerns over credibility. The news media has suffered more than its share of black eyes, figuratively. There have been revelations of reporters making up stories, fabricating details and reporting interviews that never took place, sometimes with imaginary people.

There are many examples.

A reporter named Janet Cooke at the *Washington Post* won a Pulitzer Prize for a story about an eight-year-old heroin addict. It was subsequently revealed that there was no such person, and Cooke resigned from the paper and was stripped of the Pulitzer.

At the venerable *New York Times*, it was discovered that Jayson Blair, a rising star in the newsroom, had made up dozens of stories, sometimes plagiarizing the work of other reporters or just downright lying in his writing.

The reputation of CBS News was shaken to the core when anchorman Dan Rather broadcast allegations on the program 60 Minutes II about George Bush's National Guard service 30 years earlier. It turned out that Rather's report, which aired during the 2004 presidential campaign, was based on unsubstantiated and questionable documents. Faced with intense criticism and an investigation, Rather announced within a month that he would step down as anchorman of the CBS Evening News.

And then there was Stephen Glass, who admitted making up sources and whole news stories while a staff reporter for the *New Republic* magazine.

The technology bubble of the late 1990s was also a sobering experience for the media. Many reporters were sucked into the hype and convinced by the over-blown claims of tech's high flyers. There was fierce competition between news organizations to report the latest developments, even when they lacked substance and validation. In the end, most if not all of the claims turned out to be nothing more than hot air.

The irresponsible actions of a few people in the media have injured the reputations of otherwise outstanding and conscientious news organizations.

In most cases, respected news organizations acted quickly to understand what went wrong with their internal standards of checks and balances and to take corrective action. So what we have today is a news media that has expeditiously conducted a responsible job of reexamination and is keenly aware of its responsibility as guardians of fair, accurate, responsible and balanced reporting.

News organizations have beefed up editorial scrutiny of stories and fact-checking as best they can within budget constraints and staffing cutbacks. Internally, questions are asked if a story seems too dramatic, too bold, too leading edge. Outwardly, the media has learned to smell hype coming their way from several miles away and avoid it like the plague.

Therein lies the fundamental challenge of media relations today—how to credibly communicate what your organization wants to say to its public audiences or stakeholders via the media while, at the same time, understanding the ever-changing and often trendy needs and methods of the news business. Media relations methods that seemed to work a few years ago may not achieve any results today.

Media relations requires persistence and fresh approaches. It certainly is not in any organization's best interest to adopt an attitude toward the media that might be perceived as arrogant or pushy.

Veteran Washington, DC, reporter Lyle Denniston says "a 'savior of the world' or 'working for the good of all of us' complex is always unconvincing. I am never persuaded that, as General Motors goes, so goes the nation.

"The competition of conflicting private interests reflects the openness of American society. As a journalist, however, I say just tell me what you're up to; you do not need to assume that I agree with your agenda in order to expect me to treat it with professional respect."

Many journalists simply are skeptical of public relations people, perhaps fearing hidden agendas. "PR people need to be less controlling and manipulative," says veteran network television correspondent John Laurence.

In many ways, communications to the news media mirrors behavior. An organization that dodges facts and manipulates issues will, ultimately, erode whatever credibility it may have. On the other hand, a leader in any given industry will be distinguished by how well it communicates with the media in an open, candid and professional manner.

Arthur Page—vice president of public relations at AT&T for two decades and the public relations professional after whom the Arthur Page Society was named—wrote, "all business in a democratic country begins with public permission and exists by public approval."

Page viewed media relations as the art of developing, understanding and communicating character—both corporate and individual.

And today, the six Page Principles that help to define integrity in media relations are deceptively simple:

- Tell the truth

- Prove it with action

- Listen to the audience

- Manage for tomorrow

- Conduct public relations as if the whole organization depends on it

- Remain calm, patient and good-humored

Linda Stasi, long-time columnist for the *New York Post*, candidly sums it up this way—"Be honest, be friendly and be funny. We know and you know that you're there to sell something I probably don't want, so be upfront about it. Never, never oversell or lie. If you do, remember, the reporter is the one with the last word—and that word will be in ink and read (hopefully) by many people. The best PR people are people who are honest, and in many, many cases are people who have become my friends."

Honesty and integrity are qualities that leaders and those responsible for media relations need to own and communicate tirelessly throughout their organizations, through words and deeds. Effective media relations begins with words as well as actions that are accurate, comprehensive and formed by integrity.

The Media's Lemming Effect

Ever wonder why so many stories you first read in this morning's paper show up later on the evening television newscast with little or no update? And have you ever wondered why that interesting story you heard on National Public Radio a couple of weeks ago is just now making it into the newspaper?

There exists a pecking order in America's news media. Let's draw an analogy to the much-maligned Alaskan lemming, the rodent creature that according to popular myth runs in packs, first in one direction then the other, seemingly without rhyme or reason—even if headed over a cliff. Ah, but there is rhyme and reason in the news media. There are some in the pack more trusted than others.

Despite all the appearances of competition between America's print and broadcast news media, what is covered by the news media and the style in which it is covered is largely influenced by how someone else in the news media has previously reported the story. For lack of a better description, we can call this the "lemming effect." It's all about leadership and a hierarchy of influence within the news media.

This effect shows up most often in the area of enterprise news reporting—the side of journalism that requires digging for unusual angles, finding outstanding sources and unearthing award-winning stories. Enterprise stories are generally found first on National Public Radio news programs or on the pages of major daily newspapers. Television news, in most cases, has accepted the default job of reporting the follow-up on the original story and, whenever possible, making it as sensational as possible.

Here's how it works.

Even though television news has been around a half a century and is perhaps the most powerful of the news media, the decision makers of TV news are an insecure group. With few exceptions, they will not consider running any story that smacks of controversy until it has appeared first in print, either in a newspaper or on a wire service.

One of the reasons is an unspoken fear that a story might upset an advertiser.

At the morning story planning sessions at each of the television networks in New York, producers sit around the room with copies of that day's *New York Times* in their laps. What appears in the morning *Times* often influences what America will see nine hours later on the evening television news.

It is no different in local television newsrooms in communities around the country. What will appear on the evening news is influenced by that morning's local newspaper. And stories that appeared overnight on the Associated Press broadcast wire service often provide ideas for local coverage later that day. Consequently, much of what viewers see at the end of the day is recycled old news, often from the day before.

Sure, there are exceptions, such as breaking news. The network news operations have wars, natural disasters and news conferences to cover during the day. Local news covers fires, car wrecks and local news conferences. But even then, television news is astonishingly slow to update a breaking story.

Remember when parts of the northeast, including New York City, were hit by a massive electrical power failure one hot August afternoon in 2003? Television news was all over the story, except that the next afternoon, CNN was still recycling the hardships people were facing 24 hours earlier.

On the second day of such a widespread power outage, a viewer might expect CNN and the others to tell us the latest news. Not so. They were still focusing on what happened the day before.

And it has always been thus. As a young network news correspondent starting out at CBS News, I was counseled by Zeke Segal, a highly respected veteran assignment editor, to never get ahead of the story. He advised to always get "validation" of any major story by how it would be approached by the print news media. "We [meaning, TV News] are and will always be the reaction side of journalism," he said.

Sadly, that's still true today, and the effect is compounded by the fact that contemporary television news is entertainment-driven. And, in many cities, "entertainment" news has the distinct flavor of "Amateur Hour." Far too many of today's television anchors are nothing more than actors or readers with no journalistic training or credentials. Behind the scenes are news producers and interns with varying degrees of experience who are learning on the job. It is not surprising that accuracy of reporting and the quality of writing on local television news are mediocre.

And it's not surprising that TV news people feel "safer" about airing a story once they've seen it in print somewhere.

Despite impressive technological resources that enable them to cover the news virtually anywhere on the planet, television news does little original or enterprising reporting, focusing instead on recycling whatever appeared in the newspapers or wire services.

Now, what about National Public Radio and newspapers? Whether at NPR headquarters in Washington or at their local stations around the country, a hallmark of National Public Radio is responsible, comprehensive and compelling original journalistic reporting. Many NPR junkies have forgotten the number of times they have been late to morning meetings at work because of sitting in their cars to hear the end of some story on the radio.

National Public Radio is one of America's most influential news sources, and they have the audience numbers to prove it. NPR audience statistics will often eclipse major network television news programs.

And among the rest of us who are often spellbound by some story we hear on NPR are newspaper reporters, who are looking for story ideas. If it catches their interest, there's a good chance they might write about it. And, then, of course, the TV news people read about it in the paper and the news recycling continues.

In media relations, a basic objective is to get your story before target audiences as responsibly and accurately as possible through the credible and influential conduit of the news media. You also want a reasonable degree of control over the story. And, of course, you hope for good coverage. Consequently, television news is not the first place to take your story if you hope to have it air in an accurate manner.

You want to capitalize on the perception that when the media reports about you, you are seen as a leader. Consequently, when possible and appropriate, work with public radio stations, commercial news/talk radio stations, newspapers and wire services. There, you generally will find today's best level of journalism that will lead to more credibility and influence on important audiences.

RULES OF
ENGAGEMENT

Earned Versus Paid Media

Buy an ad, and that's "paid" media. Just another word for advertising.

Talk a reporter into doing a story, and that's "earned" media. You went out, pitched a story and earned the coverage. Good for you!

There have long been lines of separation between earned and paid media—until recently. Today, some enterprising, generally smaller, newspapers and online journalistic outfits have turned to selling so-called news coverage. I guess the rationale is that when they are struggling for income, journalistic ethics can be compromised. As a result, the traditional lines of separation between advertising and news have at times gotten blurry.

A shopping mall wants recognition for writing a check and "getting involved" in worthwhile local community events. They want a photo of their general manager shaking hands with local civic leaders, and they want a story that quotes them saying self-congratulatory things that, they hope, will make them look like they are giving back to the town in which they do business.

A news story? Hardly! It's self-serving fluff that most editors would ignore. In fact, if you push most responsible editors too hard on the subject, it will come back and hurt you when you do have legitimate news.

Yet a growing number of generally smaller newspapers—squeezed by shrinking traditional advertising revenues—will sell space, usually on a special page in the paper, where businesses can run self-promotional pieces that they hope readers will think is news. News? Who are they kidding?! It's advertising, and readers can smell it across the room. And the paper wonders why their readers develop the perception that they are nothing more than an advertising rag?

I'm always a little baffled when I hear of such practices because it would be so much more credible and effective for a business to invest those same dollars to work with a professional public relations person and come up with a legitimate news angle for the media. That's earned media coverage, the good stuff.

Here's a little exercise—carefully read the front page of a major daily newspaper. And, as you do, consider that at least half of the news content was influenced by a professional public relations person who got a client involved in a story, either by providing expert perspective and being quoted or by providing background and information that brought credibility to the story. The PR people who specialize in that kind of media relations earn the respect of both clients and journalists, alike.

Perception Is the Highest Form of Reality

Perception is the most powerful force in communications. We make decisions based on how we perceive something or someone. And no two perceptions are exactly alike. We can be poles apart in our perception of something, and both be "right" because our perceptions define our reality.

During our individual life journeys, we each have endless learning experiences and challenges that influence our perceptions.

You and I see a cloud. It reminds you of the Wyeth painting of a giant with a club; to me, it looks like rain coming. Two different perceptions, both correct.

The dictionary defines "perception" as "intuitive recognition of a truth." In fact, perception is far more complex, intangible and fragile than that.

When jockeying to capture audience awareness, too many companies look for a basic truth—or "reality"—in hopes it will set their organization apart from others: "we're the *leading*" or "the *largest*...."

Unfortunately when they do that, they join an enormous universe of other organizations saying the same thing. It's a boast that won't cut through competitive clutter.

The conscious and subconscious factors that influence perception have been debated for centuries by academics and philosophers and more recently, and from a less skilled perspective, by marketing communications professionals. And, still, your perception of something tomorrow might be different than it is today and changed today from what it was yesterday. That's human nature and the nature of perceptions. We perceive events, people, companies, products and things in different ways, and we each are motivated by our individual perceptions.

Not surprisingly, understanding perception is critically important in practicing media relations today. We want to, of course, strive for accuracy and clarity in what we tell the media, reducing chances for confusion and misperceptions. We may both be right when we see different things in the cloud, but in media and public relations, the perception that counts is that of the media.

Here's an example—If you have a policy that all comments to the media need to be cleared by an attorney, then you could be building a perception with reporters of being defensive, that you've got something to hide.

The same is true if you read from a prepared statement in response to routine questions from reporters. Whether accurately or not, you are sending a signal of defensiveness. If your organization is already in hot water, you don't want to exacerbate the situation by acting evasive.

Here are six things a company, individual or organization can do to change perception:

- Get outside yourself—look at your image challenge from the perspective of an outsider, such as a client or customer or investor or the media.

- Walk into the future—define how you want your organization to be described two or three years from now by people who are important to your company.

- Challenge conventional thinking—just because it seemingly felt good a couple of years ago doesn't mean it will work in today's highly competitive arenas.

- Avoid "committee speak"—defining the perception by committee often results in too many words that say too little, too vaguely.

- Stay away from overused 50-cent marketing words—you know what they are, the dull adjectives pulled off the shelf when we can't think of anything else. Words like "unique," "innovative" and "leading provider."

- Be consistent. Once you have decided what to say and how to say it, stick with that consistent approach in working with the news media. Consistency works to build trust and helps to overcome confusion that can adversely influence an otherwise good perception.

In media relations, it doesn't matter whether you are the "largest" or the "best." If you are perceived as an organization that is communicating openly, candidly and clearly then you are sending positive signals to your audiences, including the news media. It helps you to be perceived as a winner.

Nothing Is Secret

In today's world of e-mail, the Internet and instant messaging, it's folly to think that anything is secret. Documents, notes from meetings, anything—regardless of the level of confidentiality—can be sent across town or around the world in a flash, with a single click of a mouse. It happens all the time.

In media relations, the moment you sit down to write any document—whether a news release or strategic plan—it's important to keep in mind that whatever you draft could become public, even inadvertently. Nothing is secret.

What happened at the Washington, DC, zoo is classic.

Under Dr. Lucy Spelman's watch as director of the National Zoo in Washington, DC, nearly two dozen animals, including some rare and endangered species, died and some veterinary records were changed after the fact. In one case, a popular elephant died at an early age of tuberculosis for lack of an easily obtainable vaccination. In another case, two rare zebras died from hypothermia and malnutrition. It all came to light through a series of reports in the *Washington Post*.

How did the *Post* know? Somebody talked. A front-page story by Henri E. Cauvin had all the grisly details:

"In a confidential strategy paper produced by [the public relations firm] Hill & Knowlton, the zoo is urged to be open with the media but aggressive in containing any fallout from the deaths. The 23-page plan warns that continuing inquiries by the *Washington Post* could emerge as a story of national import, creating a crisis that would imperil the zoo's bid for full accreditation and threaten the job of Director Lucy H. Spelman.

"'Lucy Spelman's credibility as a leader may appear to be diminished, with possible requests for her removal,' Hill & Knowlton says in a list of potential scenarios that could follow more 'negative news stories' on the zoo."

What happened was that Dr. Spelman paid a PR firm $50,000 to try to clean up her image. It created a perception that good PR was more important than taking responsible and affirmative steps to assure the safe welfare of zoo animals. Zoo employees were outraged by her behavior and confidential documents got into the hands of a reporter. The resulting *series* of stories portrayed Dr. Spelman as an inept zoo director and Hill & Knowlton as a shallow-minded PR firm.

It didn't stop there. The arrogance of the zoo's leader resulted in a *Washington Post* editorial that begin this way—"If only the animals could talk, we might learn more troubling truths about their care and feeding at the National Zoo. Incomplete or altered veterinary records have obscured instances of apparent neglect, misdiagnosis and other serious mistakes in connection with the deaths of at least 23 animals...."

Nothing—absolutely nothing—can be kept secret. The more egregious the sin, the more likely it will make it to the media. Remember the infamous "Deep Throat" of Nixon's Watergate, the Pentagon papers that a courageous Daniel Ellsberg released to the *New York Times* and all the exposed cover-ups? That was over 30 years ago, long before e-mail, blogs (short for "Web logs or Web journals"), the Internet and a 24-hour news cycle. Secrecy is much harder today.

Although you can't expect anything to be secret forever, there are things you can do to maximize your chances. Here are some tips on handling information before it gets public:

- Label a draft as a draft. When writing a document, such as a news release and media briefing document, type "DRAFT" at the top of the first page. Include draft version number, date and your own initials. Then, if the document becomes public prematurely, your organization has a legitimate defense that the document was a draft, not a final statement.

- Avoid e-mailing everyone. It's a bad habit at many organizations to include extraneous people on e-mails. Limit e-mail daisy chains. Especially on issues of your organization's image and reputation, only share e-mails and documents between people who are relevant to the topic.

- Have signed confidentiality statements. Employees will often think twice before leaking sensitive material when they've signed a confidentiality statement that clearly spells out that termination may result from intentionally telling secrets.

Of course, if you've invested the time to develop personal relationships with the reporters who cover your organization, that's the best safeguard in handling leaks. You will have developed credibility with the news media that will no doubt eclipse that of the informant.

There's nothing better in a potentially hostile media environment than to be on a first-name basis with key reporters. Having an established, trusted relationship with the news media can turn around wrong impressions, correct misinformation, help defuse a possibly unfavorable story and provide better and more accurate perspective for journalists.

There Is No Such Thing as "No Comment"

If you are facing some tough issues that you will asked about by the media, and you want to shout "No Comment!" why not just hold up a big red sign that says "Guilty!" The end result would be about the same. It is simply irresponsible for a spokesperson to say "no comment" because it will usually result in more damage.

During 30 years as a journalist and strategic communications consultant, I can't tell you the number of times I've seen bad situations get worse because a spokesperson decided to say—usually in a curt tone of voice—"no comment" to the media rather than find a better response.

It usually happens because some attorney mandates that the company say nothing but "no comment." That's downright dumb, it's irresponsible and it shows disregard for an organization's brand and reputation.

"The worst type of public relations person, usually found in-house at some organization, is the one who refuses to comment," says Jon Ashworth of the *Times* in London.

"No comment" suggests guilt, arrogance and abruptness, all the emotional elements you want to avoid during a super-charged situation. It implies you have something to hide. Whatever the level of desperation, frustration and aggravation when things go bad, those two words are never an option.

Here is an alternative approach to handling a potentially damaging situation for your organization:

First, when the phone rings and it's a reporter calling you, remember that there is no law that says you must talk with the reporter at that moment. If you feel unprepared or ambushed, buy some time to collect your thoughts and think of something to say. Explain to the reporter that you are more than happy to speak with him or her but you are in the middle of something. Ask if he or she is on deadline and negotiate a reasonable time frame to return the call, such as a half-hour to one hour.

Next—and this is essential—ask the reporter to give you an idea of what he or she wants to talk about. Never ask reporters what questions they are going to ask; just query the subject matter. Most reporters will work with you. Then, get together with your public relations people and others to formulate a meaningful statement other than "no comment." Buying some time is an invaluable tool in media relations because it allows you to get over being nervous about talking with a reporter, possibly over an adverse issue, and helps you to focus. Finally, and this is really important, contact the reporter as promised.

If your organization is facing an unfavorable situation that might draw media questions, it is essential to work in advance of any media contact and develop a response or statement, no matter how brief it might be. Think of it as a good opportunity to try to turn around a negative perception. A possible response could begin something like this: "While we are not prepared to make a formal statement at this time…" and then bridge to one or two brief messages about the situation that you believe are important. In that way, you are giving the impression of being responsive and responsible.

Lastly, remember that it's okay to be brief. In fact, the fewer words the better as long as they are not "no comment." The media will live with a response that's only a sentence or two because you are taking the time to at least say *something* during a difficult time. Consider a response that might elicit sympathy—"While this is a challenging time, we wanted to say…"—and again bridge to a brief message.

Whether you feel it or not, show genuine sincerity and a willingness to communicate. A positive attitude often will communicate as much as actual words. It may be your only constructive option.

If faced with a developing, possibly negative situation, why not say, "We want to be clear and accurate in anything we say. We are still gathering information that we will share with you when we have the whole picture."

In other words, there are many things you can say to the news media rather than "no comment." Those two words are not an option.

View an adverse situation as an opportunity to briefly deliver positive messages that communicate responsiveness and concern.

Off-the-Record Versus Background

The first thing to remember is that there is really no such thing as an "off-the-record" comment, particularly if you want to maintain some level of credibility. Strictly speaking, "off the record" means that nothing you have to say can be reported by a journalist. Nothing. In that case there is no reason to be having the conversation.

If you have something to share with the news media, there is no reason it should ever be considered off the record. I know many journalists who will smartly refuse to allow interviewees to go off the record during an interview. When you talk off the record, integrity can be compromised and enduring trust in a relationship with the media put to the test. The best advice is to avoid any off-the-record situation.

On the other hand, background briefings without attribution to a specific source have become commonplace, particularly in political and government circles. Background briefings are a valuable tool in media relations today. We hear and read all the time statements like "…according to White House sources," or "Military commanders say…."

Background briefings are helpful to the news media to provide perspective and depth of understanding about an issue, event or story. A reliable source is providing information yet the name of the source really isn't important to the story.

A word of caution—background briefings with the news media can be fraught with hazards. Anything you say in a background briefing can be reported, so there must be additional ground rules clearly agreed upon in advance. For example, in the background briefing, the name of your organization could be used unless you specify otherwise. Another risk is that you might forget to ask reporters not to use your name or job title.

If you have told a reporter that you will provide background without attribution, then whatever you say can be reported but your name will not be used. If you forget to set the boundaries then anything is fair game.

The Value of an Apology

I have never failed to be impressed by how a simple, honest apology can defuse the most volatile situation, often averting a crisis communications problem for a corporation or politician.

In another time, in the cowboy film *She Wore a Yellow Ribbon*, John Wayne growled "never apologize and never explain." But that was then, over 50 years ago in a macho western. This is now. Today, apologies can do wonders.

Consider this example. "Gov. John Rowland changed his story Friday and acknowledged that friends—including some under suspicion in a federal corruption investigation—paid for work on his summer home," reported Susan Haigh of the Associated Press. "Rowland's admission, made public *in a statement* (emphasis added), came 10 days after he insisted he alone had paid for improvements on the house at Bantam Lake."

Another politician confirms what we believe about most politicians—that they accept payoffs. Yet, in this case, Rowland exacerbates his situation by lying and then changing his story and announcing it in a written *statement*. A *statement*! Who's going to believe a written statement? Why not just come clean and stand up in front of the microphones and reporters with notebooks and say something that begins with "I've made a terrible mistake, and I'm going to do everything possible to make it right...." (Rowland was later found guilty.)

Equally astonishing is the absolute refusal by some organizations and titans of industry to ever admit to any mistakes, even when their hands are caught in the cookie jar. In fact, it seems that the larger the scope of misdoings and egregious misconduct, the more likely that arrogance will prevent the perpetrators from even considering the value of an apology.

Did you ever hear an apology from Enron, Global Crossing or World-com? The message we heard was one of blame and excuses, seemingly driven by greed and arrogance. We were left with the impression that many of those titans of business were just well-compensated crooks.

Another example: Hurricane Isabel cut a destructive swath up the east coast of the United States, leaving hundreds of thousands of people with no power for days. Several of the power companies were slow to restore service. It was disclosed in the media that they had cut back investment in the number of repair crews needed to upgrade power lines in order to show a better bottom line to investors.

Rather than standing up in a news conference and saying simply, "We made a mistake, we apologize and we are now working feverishly to restore electricity to your homes," the power company executives attempted to defend their decisions. They did battle with the news media. They made the media their enemy rather than saying they screwed up. It was classic John Wayne behavior, circa 1950. Yet, today it came off as incompetent and sounded like emphasis on greed over a clear focus on customer service. It wasn't smart, and the companies were broiled by the public, the media, politicians and…investors.

There are unfortunately far too many executives and attorneys who choose to duke it out (pun intended) with tough stances. The worse the situation, the greater the arrogance, and, often, the greater the media feast of one story after another. Denying responsibility or twisting facts, especially in the face of evidence to the contrary, will actually create a news story. Hey, just apologize, make amends, move forward.

We are human, we do our best, we are not perfect, we make honest mistakes. In extremely difficult times, an effective and proven method of controlling media relations is by way of an apology.

A Gas Station Mentality

This is a true story—the marketing communications staff at a major software company was stumped, trying to figure out how to describe a new product that was being rushed to market after a competitor beat them to the punch. What could they say to capture the media's attention about their product? How could they create clever positioning. Words failed.

So, their boss got a brilliant idea—he instructed his staff to check the competitor's Web site and see how they had described their new product and then…kinda, sorta plagiarize that description. Sound familiar? Unfortunately, it's all too familiar in the technology industry. And it's a recipe for more failure. It's a strategy for landing yourself in second place…or worse.

Everyone—the financial markets, investors, venture capitalists and all of us ordinary people—likes technology because it's exciting, it makes our lives easier and more manageable, and when a company with substance comes along, technology can be a fun investment. And yet, the high technology world, with few exceptions, is too often a vast wasteland of blandness when it comes to distinctive and imaginative marketing communications and media relations.

No one is certain why, but technology has traditionally been wrapped up in talking about itself, using words that may sound impressive but mean little or nothing. "Technobabble," as one reporter called it.

Take a closer look at all the failed technological pioneers and, with few exceptions, you will find companies that pretty much used the same words and jargon to say the same things, regardless of their product or service. How many times have you heard phrases like "the world's leading innovative integrated solutions provider…."

It's a lot like gas stations—when one gas station opens at an intersection, others follow, promoting themselves in the same way, saying the same thing. It's all copycat. Same with technology—when one tech company promotes itself with tired 50-cent marketing words, others copy. The rest of us, seeing nothing authentic, get bored and lose interest.

Nowhere is it more prevalent than in the information technology or "IT" sector. It seems like everyone is an "IT" company, from business consultants to software companies to banks to your local newspaper. It's a catch-all phrase for companies that can't figure out how to explain what they do. Remember the 1980s habit of stores calling themselves such things as "Kitchenware...*and more*"? Today, it's "IT and more."

But despite all of this, technology not only holds the promise for America's success and security, it has the opportunity to be an enduring Wall Street darling. So, here's an easy four-step checklist to help you authentically trumpet the true value of your enterprise and separate the leaders from the losers:

- Think and talk outside of yourself—Invest the time in some high level strategic thinking to define how you want your company talked about in two or three years.

- Make that strategic vision come alive—Develop an original strategic plan that credibly achieves what's called "competitive positioning."

- Stand in your customer's shoes—Learn how to communicate the value of your product or service to the person who ultimately makes the decision and has the authority to buy.

- Talk in soundbites, not "elevator speeches"—A soundbite is describing your endeavor, precisely, in one breath (about 16 seconds), using words that are understandable, credible, exciting and memorable. An elevator speech (what you could tell someone about your company in the time it takes to reach your floor), although popular, takes too long. Reporters, distracted by others who can say it better, will lose interest.

When used properly, these principles of effective communications work not just for technology companies but for any organization.

The challenge is to overcome a common thread among most companies—the inability to incisively and concisely describe their individual value and what's genuinely special about what they deliver to their audiences, their customers. Too often, it's stalled in its own words.

Technology and many other industry sectors occasionally run out of gas and desperately need to fill their tanks. With high octane. Then, a wash and wax. And then, get back out on the racetrack with timely and compelling communications.

Hiding Behind Paper

Perhaps one of the most common "sins" of public relations and communications people is never actually doing the work to identify how to bridge the gap between what is *newsworthy* for the media to consider and the promotional message you are pushing on behalf of a client or employer.

Consequently, too many (if not most) media campaigns are centered around—maybe it's more accurate to say "hidden behind"—a systematic flood of news releases and expensive media materials that are sent out "carpet-bomb" style to the media, often to the wrong people.

If there is one common trait among many people who are charged with media relations, it is a reluctance to actually interface with the media in any way, such as through a phone call. Too many public relations people hide behind news releases, media lists, mailings, bulk e-mails and faxes, never actually picking up the phone to speak with a journalist and develop a working relationship.

"Don't overwhelm the assignment desk and producers with too much information," counsels C-SPAN's Steve Scully. "With all the paperwork we deal with everyday, less is better. Accurate and *timely* is required."

The conventional wisdom among PR people that "more is better" is both ineffective in contemporary media relations and annoying to journalists. Effective media relations today mandates approaching the right journalist with the right story angle. And it requires a personal contact rather than hiding behind paper.

A general manager of a public radio station tells friends she has built a terrific library at home with all the books sent to her over the years by book publicists who never took the time to make a phone call and figure out who to send a book to in order to schedule an interview on the air for the author. She got on the publicity mailing list and received a ton of books. The general manager (or station manager), by the way, is never the right person to contact.

On that subject, certainly many public and news/talk radio stations are interested in interviewing authors about new books on timely issues but you will find that each program has a producer designated to review and consider possible interviews. It's the responsibility of a public relations person to find those stations in respective markets, identify which programs to approach and make an initial phone call to the right producer to ask how they prefer to be pitched about a possible interview. You will find they all have individual styles and preferences and that a phone call is a valuable first step toward developing what can be a lasting relationship.

At a TV newsroom in Denver, they still remember the time when a local law firm representing billionaire Philip Anschutz faxed in a 17-page news release about 30 minutes before airtime for the early evening newscast. The fax cover page demanded that the news release be read...verbatim. Not surprisingly, the program producer ignored the entire news release. A hot exchange later erupted between the news producer and one of the attorneys after the attorney called demanding an explanation of why the release wasn't mentioned on the air.

Jon Ashworth, business features editor at the *Times* of London, says, "I am constantly being 'pitched' with ideas for soft articles that are often just glorified ads. The PR agencies are putting in the calls so that they can tick names off a list—part of justifying their fee. I find this a waste of everyone's time. Overall, most journalists see PR people as a necessary evil."

PR representatives as a general rule are aggressive in cranking out news releases and dutifully sending a blizzard of them out to as many journalists as possible. Yet, they rarely make any sort of personal follow-up contact with the media or are responsive if (holy smokes!) a reporter actually calls for more information if the news release catches their eye.

That's particularly the style of PR people in the book or tourism promotion business. They send out paper or e-mail news releases to massive, generalized and seldom-updated media lists, then apparently go to lunch. Countless reporters have complained that the ball is dropped at that point.

A major international agency, for example, "represents" a venerable old resort in Virginia and blindly sends out news releases. But when a reporter calls the agency, they always get voice mail and messages left are not returned.

Reporters say that book publicists are also among the most lethargic. They send review copies of books with news releases neatly tucked inside the front cover to seemingly every journalist on the planet. But call one of the publicists back to ask for a photo of the author to be e-mailed to you or to excerpt a chapter and you might as well be talking to a brick wall.

Walk into the newsroom of any daily newspaper or television station when the mail arrives, and you will be amazed at the volume of unsolicited paper—news releases, media kits and boxes of promotional stuff—that shows up.

At *USA Today*, for example, where editors are required to read, however briefly, everything that comes in, the mailroom guys cart it in, using wheeled garbage cans that are piled high with paper. It's a conga train of garbage cans. Some of the mail is addressed merely to "Occupant, Newsroom," and that's usually the first to be pitched out. The staff makes jokes about it being recycled into fireplace logs.

In fairness, much of the unsolicited news material is addressed to the "Editor" or someone at the news organization by name. But too often, media materials are addressed to someone who moved to another news outfit, and in some cases, to someone who died, years ago.

Typical news media materials begin with a form-type generic cover letter that explains the critical importance of the news from the sender's perspective. The letters generally have an urgent "stop the presses!" tone about them and suggest that this news is the greatest announcement since Al Gore supposedly invented the Internet. More often than not, the cover letter fails to suggest how this "news" might actually be made into a news story. Sadly for their creators, these news materials are pushed aside by items that carry a more genuine tone or are more professionally presented.

Most journalists prefer a specific, personalized story pitch rather than a news release—"an idea that is news driven," as so many news people have said, rather than a typical fluffy news release.

"Give me numbers, think of other possible sources and even give sources who might be on the other side. That is really helpful. What is the controversial point, who might we want to talk to on the other side," says a wire service reporter.

Pat Piper produced The Larry King Show for over a decade on Mutual Radio and today collaborates with King on a variety of books. He thinks most PR people oversell to the media and compulsively send too much "stuff."

"Here's a newsflash," Piper says. "The world may revolve around your client but the world I deal with doesn't usually include your client or cause. I always have a trash can when I open the mail. I always have a delete when I read an e-mail attachment."

Denver talk show host and former ABC Network News correspondent Greg Dobbs gives this useful advice—"Ask yourself what the media wants and needs. The answer won't necessarily be the message you want to communicate, but if you don't get them "in the door," the strongest message on earth will have no impact.

"How do you figure out what the media wants and needs? Simple: pretend you are a reporter, and your only stake in the matter is in getting a good story, not in getting your message out. In other words, put yourself in the reporter's shoes and offer what he or she is looking for. In short, get their attention, then work on carving that message."

Media relations is not blitzing everyone in the newsroom with the same news release or media kit. It all comes down to establishing a relationship—making a phone call to the news organization, identifying the right reporter, developing a credible and balanced news pitch and delivering that pitch in the brief and incisive manner that reporters prefer.

Stick to the News

This chapter is about a misguided trend by some corporations and organizations—call it a bad habit—of using news releases and other materials intended to support working with the news media to manipulate credibility. It's about "safe harbor" statements, which are tantamount to saying "nothing you are about to read is true," and "about" statements, which are blatant self-promotion. Both adversely impact credibility in dealing with the news media.

The idea of including in news releases a piece of legal language called a "safe harbor" statement started in the mid-1990s with high technology companies. Their attorneys believed the companies needed protection from themselves and from many of the often outlandish claims they made in releases and other promotional materials. In other words, their own attorneys questioned whether the bravado of tech companies was truthful.

So, they came up with standard safe harbor language, or boilerplate, to be included at the end of every news release, that they hoped would legally protect a company from being accused of outright lying. Here's an example of a safe harbor statement from a technology company:

> *This press release may include statements that may constitute "forward-looking statements," including its estimates of future business prospects or financial results and statements containing the words "believe," "estimate," "project," "expect" or similar expressions. Forward-looking statements inherently involve risks and uncertainties that could cause actual results of this company and its subsidiaries (collectively, the "Company") to differ materially from the forward-looking statements. Factors that could contribute to such differences include: the ability of the Company to implement and achieve widespread customer acceptance of its Report Services software on a timely basis; the Company's ability to recognize deferred revenue through delivery of products or satisfactory performance of services; contin-*

ued acceptance of the Company's products in the marketplace; the timing of significant orders; delays in the Company's ability to develop or ship new products; market acceptance of new products; competitive factors; general economic conditions; currency fluctuations; and other risks detailed in the Company's registration statements and periodic reports filed with the Securities and Exchange Commission. By making these forward-looking statements, the Company undertakes no obligation to update these statements for revisions or changes after the date of this release.

In 186 words, a company suggests "reader, beware!" It's classic "C-Y-A." A journalist takes one look and understandably wonders whether anything in the news release is true. (By the way, I decided not to spell-out "C-Y-A" because this is a "G"-rated book.)

And, then, there are the "about" statements, like mini-advertisements within news releases.

Over the objections of many in the news business, "about" statements have become common in many news releases. They are generally lengthy, boastful boilerplate describing great things "about" the company or organization. It's self-serving ego stuff that impresses few people, certainly few journalists.

Here's an example of a typical "about" statement, this one from People-Soft:

PeopleSoft (Nasdaq: PSFT) is the world's leading provider of application software for the real-time enterprise. PeopleSoft pure Internet software enables organizations to reduce costs and increase productivity by directly connecting customers, suppliers, partners and employees to business processes on-line, in real time. PeopleSoft's integrated, best-in-class applications include Customer Relationship Management, Supply Chain Management, Human Capital Management, Financial Management and Application Integration. Today more than 5,200 organizations in 140 countries run on PeopleSoft software.

Journalists say it's easy enough to get background information from an organization's Web site, so companies should just need to focus on "news" in a news release.

This seems logical, but corporate rationale, with an eye always on sales and promotion, takes a different view at many organizations. The position seems to be "if our attorneys think we're going to the edge of believability anyway, we might as well go all the way and use news releases for sales purposes."

In companies where public relations is under the control of the marketing department, the trend of marrying "about" and safe harbor statements has gotten completely out of control. Software developer MicroStrategy, for example, includes a voluminous 200-word boilerplate "about," at the end of its news releases, full of puffy adjectives trumpeting the company's glory. They are by no means alone.

"About" boilerplate is a trend that has become common place at too many organizations who apparently are under the impression that news releases are just another type of sales collateral material.

What they didn't realize is that news releases are targeted for the news media, not potential customers. News releases are not sales brochures or advertisements or billboards. News releases are intended to announce legitimate news.

After all, what's the purpose of the news release? To communicate legitimate news or distribute promotional fluff? If the latter, consider protecting your organization's credibility by passing the assignment off to the marketing department and advise them to buy an ad.

Veteran C-Span television producer Scott Scully wants news releases that are credible and concise. "Send *accurate* information to the assignment desk," he says. "This means the correct date and time…contact person and *relevant* information."

News releases can be most effective when used to announce timely and relevant information that affects an organization's audiences. In today's highly competitive world, where the image of an organization rests on credible and accurate words, too much is at stake to mess with credibility by bastardizing a news release for self-promotional agendas.

It all comes back to the traditional intent of a news release, that bridge for communicating with the news media, and understanding, above all, that a release is all about telling accurate news and helping journalists develop a story.

If the news release content is accurate, truthful and timely, there is no journalistic or legal reason for a safe harbor statement. Just tell the "news."

And about the imagined need for that "about" boilerplate in a news release, let's get real. The unique value and competitive positioning of any company, organization, issue or cause on the planet can be described in fewer than a dozen "quotable" and memorable words, easily included as a phrase within the actual news release copy. If it drones on much longer, it becomes a speech.

Over and over, journalists say that the best form of media relations is relationship-based, when a person responsible for media relations simply stays in touch with a circle reporters who are interested in their organization. As we have stated earlier in this book, news releases are no substitute for getting to know the right journalists.

News releases are to announce news, not to be used as advertising flyers. Always tell the truth, and you won't need to hide behind an attorney or a safe harbor.

Contentious Words Are Thought-Stoppers

I have always loved to read Mark Twain. About writing, he told a friend, "I notice that you use plain, simple language, short words and brief sentences. That is the way to write English—it is the modern way and the best way. Stick to it; don't let fluff and flowers and verbosity creep in. When you catch an adjective, kill it."

It has long been important to many companies and organizations to claim—especially when describing themselves in news releases—that they are "the largest" or "the best" or "the leading" or whatever.

Companies often spend enormous amounts of time trying to figure out the best words to use. They exhaust themselves with such boasting, attempting to make it stick and convince us that they are the greatest outfits on the planet.

Such contentious words seldom fly. Claiming to be the "best" will often cause a listener or reader to stop in their tracks and question whether it's true or not. They need to remember Twain's advice to kill the adjectives.

Remember all the "dot-com" and technology companies of the late 1990s? With negligible track records or earnings, they all claimed to be "the most advanced" or "the leading integrated service provider...." And where are they now? They were not believable.

If I were to tell you that I am "the smartest man on earth," your ability to listen to and believe what I was saying would likely stop at that point. I might continue talking and provide numerous reasons to support my claim, but chances are you would still be questioning the word "smartest." You wouldn't be listening to me but rather compiling a list in your mind of the many other people far smarter than me. My claim would lack credibility and everything else I might attempt to say would be dismissed.

It is a natural impulse when we hear boastful words to stop where we are and immediately question their validity. A company claims to be out-standing, and we quietly think to ourselves "Well, I can think of a dozen other companies that are better," ignoring whatever else the company tries to say.

When someone or an organization brags in the media, they are not only being contentious. They are gambling with their credibility. One single contentious word or phrase can stop effective communications.

Attorneys Speak Legalese

With full knowledge that I am entering possibly hostile waters here, I will say that, as a broad and sweeping generalization, attorneys seldom make for good spokespersons when left unchecked. Many attorneys speak primarily "legalese," a vague-sounding, ambiguous and somewhat evasive language that not a lot of us, including the news media, understand. The attorneys presumably comprehend what they are saying and other attorneys may, too. It comes from their training. But most of us don't understand. Legalese is not everyday language.

Attorneys are important and valuable partners in the news media communication process. They can give essential guidance and suggestions on wording and opinions about legal issues. They can help to identify potential minefields and problems well in advance. But the language of law needs to be translated into words, phrases and thoughts that more effectively communicate with the key audiences we are seeking to reach, inform and motivate, including the media.

In my work, both as a journalist and in public relations, I've found only a handful of attorneys who are skilled at delivering concise messages to the media in layman terms. Rather than working with communicators to find interesting ways to make things happen, so many attorneys actually impede the image and media relations efforts of their clients or companies by coming up with laundry lists of usually improbable scenarios and finding reasons why doing anything would be a bad idea.

Lawyers have a place in the media relations process. Get their counsel, consider the opportunities and think about what's best for your organization and your audiences and stakeholders. And, if you are stuck with an attorney as a spokesperson, get them some media training, *first*.

When dealing with the news media, we need to communicate as clearly and accurately as possible. Legal speak is seldom convincing in working with the media, and all too often can cause confusion by getting tangled up in its own jargon.

MEDIA RELATIONS
FIELD GUIDE

The Pillars of Media Relations

Think of the pillars of effective news media relations as three legs on a stool that allow you to stand above the crowd and be seen. Take away one or two legs, and you'll fall off. Add too many legs, and the stool becomes awkward and unmanageable. Here are the three pillars:

Pillar One—The Media Relations Plan. A plan gives focus to purpose and objectives. Why would any organization ever consider launching an outreach program, issuing a news release or making any public statement without some sort of plan that provides purpose, relevance and context?

Without a plan, public statements or promotional announcements usually lack focus and could actually work at cross-purposes with an organization's overall marketing and business objectives. You could be compromising your company's reputation. So, why would you say anything in public without a plan? I cannot think of any reason except for carelessness or ambivalence about your organization's image. Nonetheless, many companies crank out news release after news release, often without rhyme or reason.

Effective media relations begins with a carefully thought out plan to competitively position an organization. It embraces the overall corporate vision and objectives and gives focus, purpose and reason to a communications effort. It does not begin with tactics or with copying things that you've seen other people do to boost visibility in the media. It begins with asking yourself candid and tough questions that will help you really put your fingers on the distinct pulse of your organization and identify precisely the right ways and the best words to enhance your image before key audiences. Some of those questions are:

- What's so special about your organization that makes it stand out from anyone else, and who cares beyond the company parking lot?

- What are the things about your company that appeal most to the people who really matter outside and who rely on your organization, such as customers and stakeholders?

- How do you want your company talked about, in clear, jargon-free words? In other words, how do you think your best customer might describe why you were chosen over a competitor?

- And…what is genuinely *newsworthy* about your organization and what it does or produces?

Think of a media relations plan as a beacon that will guide important audiences to your organization. A media relations plan mirrors the objectives of a company's business plan and works to bring the strategic business plan to life more efficiently and more compellingly than any other method.

The plan's components are straightforward:

- Situation Overview—A few paragraphs to summarize the lay of the land, competitive environment, challenges and obstacles, advantages and opportunities.

- Audiences—A list of all audiences that you intend to reach through your media relations initiative—internal and external, public and highly specialized.

- Positioning Message—The message about your organization that should clearly differentiate you from your competitors and capture the attention of your key audiences.

- Objectives—Preferably three and certainly no more than four objectives that reflect and complement the objectives in your organization's business plan.

- Strategies—There must be a strategy for each objective. This is where you describe in detail how you intend to achieve the objectives. In other words, how you plan to get from here to there.

- Tactics—The unique and distinctive action points that will bring your strategies to life in order to achieve the objectives.

Be mindful of not allowing tactics to drive the planning process. Tactics are the fun side of planning, while objectives and strategies require more thought. Consequently, people all too often jump to tactics that may or may not be relevant to the plan. That could lead to wasted time, wrong strategic directions and costly mistakes.

Let me digress for a moment to talk about objectives, strategies and tactics and provide an example.

An objective might be where you want to go, such as to drive to the beach for the weekend.

A strategy is how you are going to make it happen, such as planning the shortest trip at the best time to avoid traffic. There is always just one strategy to achieve each objective.

Tactics are the actions, items or steps needed to bring a strategy to life and for accomplishing an end, such as, in this case, making sure the car is fueled, finding the car keys, having a roadmap and making sure the suitcase is in the trunk.

During the process of developing a plan, the right tactics will naturally reveal themselves. Chances are you can even identify clever new tactics that will become distinctive to your organization. So, even if someone else currently has an advantage on you in the area of media relations, it's realistic to gain the upper hand because many people don't bother with developing a smart media relations plan. I've found that most people think only about tactics, such as a news release, and hope that will solve everything. Before you think about tactics, think BIG. Have a strategy.

Once you've launched that process, you will begin to see your company through a new set of eyes, with 20-20 vision, focused on the essence of what's important. You will no longer find it relevant to think of your organization in terms of competitors but rather as a unique organization of talented people who are part of something big.

Pillar Two—Be Original. While it always helps to know your competition, ignore what they are saying and how they are saying it. While a competitor may do something cool, it may not be either smart or effective. If there's a news story about them, and you are not mentioned, forget it because, like the city bus, another opportunity will soon come along before you know it. If you copy or react to them, you have, by default, put yourself in second place, made yourself a "wannabe" in the media's eyes. The news media doesn't like wannabes.

Ignore how the competition talks to the media. Chart new territory. Be original and imaginative, because you are smarter and savvier than they are.

There's too much competitive clutter out there in the marketplace these days to be ordinary. Throw out "conventional wisdom" and *traditional* approaches to media relations. I've often said that "conventional wisdom" is a code phrase for dull and predictable. Challenge the claims and promises of your public relations agency, if you have one. Forget news releases and expensive media kits. Don't fall into the trap of feeling compelled to announce every little thing that happens at your place. Your organization has special things to say, so why say them in a predictable and boring fashion?

An essential part of being original is to use clever visuals. If you want to quickly leapfrog your brand out ahead of your competition, think about three things: visuals...visuals...visuals. Nothing captures the media's attention faster than great pictures. When it comes to making decisions on what gets on the air, a TV news producer most often will go with a second-class story that has great visuals over a better story without visuals. It's just the way it goes, and it's not going to change. Television news is driven completely by visuals over content.

And these days, print journalism is more focused on appealing visuals, as well. *USA Today* created a whole new way of using color, graphics, visuals and pictures when it debuted in the early 1980s, and most other newspapers and magazines have followed and improved on the trend. The fastest way into the business section of a major daily newspaper is with a story that has a compelling photo. Most business editors could not care less about the introduction of a new automobile but when the car maker's chief executive officer and his top designer are seated on the front of the car in a photo, along with a story about the clever teaming of the two executives, editors pay attention.

Pillar Three—Tell the Truth. Regardless of the situation and circumstances, accuracy and candor in dealing with the media is always the best route.

Ever since the technology bubble burst in the early part of this decade, pundits have debated the possible reasons why it happened. Certainly there were numerous financial and market forces at work, not the least of which was the massive overvaluation of many technology stock offerings, based on nothing more than a promise and a prayer. But the most fundamental reason, in my opinion, was the lack of truth in how so many tech companies were promoted to the news media.

In the rock 'n' roll environment of high-flying late 1990s technology companies, when everything—literally everything from balance sheets and business plans to marketing claims and stock performance—was overstated or nonexistent, communications with the media was also hyped. The climate was right—business reporters, bored of covering the traditional stories, were all of a sudden being hustled by exciting new companies and ideas. They took the bait and all the hype. The stories seemed too good not to believe. Everyone from venture capitalists to analysts and the markets was seemingly validating the high-flying news. Of course, as it turned out, the venture capitalists and analysts and markets were all making tons of money directly from the tech companies.

But in the end, contempt for the truth spelled downfall. Ultimately, the truth will come out. From the perspective of journalists I have spoken with, failed technology companies have no one to blame but themselves for their demise. Greed eclipsed truth and accuracy. And we have seen the fallout—the markets and investors skittish of any tech venture, even at the expense of the handful of companies out there who might be making money with a unique product or service. The once ever-so-smug leaders of tech during that era nearly killed an entire industry by not telling the truth.

In the world of effective media relations, imaginative ideas and the truth win out over conventional wisdom and hype every day of the week.

Mission Statements and Positioning Messages

A heating and air conditioning contractor handed me his card as we discussed the price of updating the system in my home. There on the bottom of his card was his company's "mission statement." It said the company had "vision," was "dedicated to serving customers" and a few other nice things, in about 18 words.

But, the card didn't say what I really wanted to know—why I should choose this company over any other heating and air conditioning outfit. That would be a "positioning message."

This company and many others proudly trumpet mission statements rather than focusing on the uniqueness of the products or services they offer. They are bragging from their perspective rather than understanding my needs.

Why, you ask, is this important to know in media relations? Because one of our primary goals in getting before the news media is to communicate a subtle differentiating message about our organization to audiences reached by the media. We not only want to be reported on but also remembered.

What's the difference between a mission statement and a positioning message? There's a big difference. Here's a guide:

A mission statement tells people who are close to your organization *specifically* and *clearly* where you want to go in a perfect world. It is visionary, idealistic and filled with words that tell people that you are nice. It describes the future, a quest for growth or a promise of unparalleled integrity. Who can argue with that? Mission statements don't, however, talk about where you are today or your competitive edge but only what you *hope* to achieve.

Mission statements are intended to target mostly internal audiences—employees, stakeholders, boards of directors and business partners. A mission statement is not a part of marketing communications or media relations.

But a positioning message focuses on today and should incisively leave an audience with a clear understanding of who you are. It describes what is distinctive about your organization that will give it a competitive advantage today. It's a simple message, not a slogan, that gets to the core of what's special about you. It is a pillar of marketing communications and media relations.

Here's a story. When I began working with leaders of 4-H on a major and ongoing initiative to reshape the image and brand of that national youth development organization, I walked into an environment that had only known mission statements and slogans. 4-H, like many other such groups, had changed their mission statement and slogan to the point where the words were so general and nondescript that they had lost all meaning. Many people knew the brand and 4-H clover logo but few had understanding of what 4-H did as an organization. 4-H lacked a positioning message, a message that would break through competitive clutter and influentially recalibrate the 4-H brand.

I believed the answer could be found by talking with the youth of 4-H around America. My strategy was to find a way to describe the unique "soul" of 4-H in words that were clear, adjective-free and left no one out.

As I traveled from state to state chatting with groups of 4-H youth and listening to how they described the 4-H adventure, I began hearing the same words being used, whether the young people were in Madison, Georgia, or Davis, California.

4-H youth were using words like "community" and "young people" (not "kids"). They said they were "learning" by working together in a mentoring environment with adults. And what were they learning? I asked. "Leadership, citizenship and life skills," they answered.

I listened to the youth of 4-H and what they told me was that "4-H is a community of young people across America who are learning leadership, citizenship and life skills." They had defined one of the strongest positioning messages I had ever heard. It said it all about America's oldest youth development organization, and it said it in clear and simple language.

Before long, the entire organization was using the positioning message. It spread like wildfire. A young 4-H girl stood at a podium for the Governor of Indiana and 300 people to dedicate remodeled 4-H buildings at the Indiana State Fair, and she began by saying "4-H is a community of young people…."

4-H youth put it on T-shirts. County agents use it on their e-mail signature lines. It is being used everywhere and at all levels of the organization. And the result is that wider audiences are becoming aware of the scope and impact of 4-H today in helping America's young people.

The positioning message sets you apart from your competitors. And here's a little tip—to sharpen your appeal, narrow your position. We cannot be all things to all people. To be successful, we must focus on one thing and be the best at it.

One thing, you say? Yes. Your organization might do many other things, but be recognized for excelling at one thing and get people talking about that, and you will win competitively.

Remember all those "And More" businesses that couldn't figure out what they were? "Windows, Doors and More." "Yarns, Sewing and More." "Electronics, Hobbies and More."

Many of those places are gone simply because they failed to build a reputation of being outstanding in one area. They tried to be all things to all people.

Wal-Mart, you might argue, is an "and more" business. Not so. Even though they may sell just about everything imaginable, the company has for decades narrowly focused on one competitive message—"Always the Lowest Price. Always." That's Wal-Mart's positioning message. In an ever-changing marketplace, they've been consistent, and they've won. Their promise has been fulfilled across America, and it has given them the edge.

Pictures Make the Story

Several years ago, my marketing communications agency was working with the marketing people at Learjet headquarters in Wichita, Kansas, on the introduction of a new business jet, the Learjet 45. Rollouts of new corporate jets had become so commonplace in Wichita that even the hometown daily newspaper, the *Wichita Eagle*, no longer saw any news value in them.

I discussed the challenge with noted photographer and former photojournalist Ed Lallo, whom I had hired to get publicity pictures of the new business jet. Ed had never before worked on an aviation project and came to town with fresh ideas on how to get a winning photo of the Learjet 45. His best idea was both daring and dangerous—to get the then-Learjet CEO, Brian Barents, to stand on top of a Learjet 45 for a photo session. My job was to talk Brian into the stunt, and he didn't let me down.

Next morning, we were out before dawn with a dew-covered Learjet 45 on a remote tarmac of Wichita airport with two cherry-picker cranes, one to hoist the CEO up on top of the jet, and the other to position Ed with all his camera gear right above the nose of the jet.

I stood in the background, noting that Brian was wearing slick-soled Italian loafers while standing on the curved and still dew-moistened top of the jet, about 20 feet in the air. There were no safety nets, and he stayed in position only through his own nerve and calm balance.

photo by Ed Lallo

Ed rapid-fired both of his cameras and got the picture he wanted within 60 seconds. Brian was carefully retrieved from his dangerous perch, and the photo shoot was complete. Next step, a quick trip to a local one-hour photo lab and a check of the negatives. Then, on to the local Associated Press office where, through Ed's personal contacts, a photo was scanned and transmitted to AP headquarters in New York.

From there, it was then sent to newspapers nationwide on the AP PhotoWire, along with a two-sentence caption I wrote that began "On Top of His World—Learjet CEO Brian Barents...." The caption trumpeted the debut of the Learjet 45 and a couple of the aircraft's special features.

Our photo with caption was picked up by more than 800 newspapers across America, making it one of the most successful promotions in the business of corporate aviation. And yes, one of those papers was the *Wichita Eagle*, which ran the photo in the middle of the front page, above the fold, the next morning. Overnight, one imaginative photo broke the mold and set a new standard for how business aircraft were promoted through the general news media.

All of a sudden, the phones at Learjet were ringing. The company had found the pulse of a whole new market of potential customers—wealthy individuals who could afford the price tag, no longer just corporations. These individuals, many of them software and technology *nouveau riche,* wanted an affordable jet. Yet until that time, they had been an elusive audience for Learjet because they had never before owned a business aircraft, and the company had no way of getting their attention.

Our work for Learjet was such a success that we soon got the photography genius of Ed Lallo involved in another event—to celebrate the merger of two railroad giants, CSX Transportation and Conrail. At the merger event in Jacksonville, Florida, there were many other things going on, including a live television program, distributed via satellite to all employees of the two railroads, as well as news conferences and receptions.

But it was Ed's visual that told the story of the success of the merger for editors at news wire services and business pages across America. He got Conrail and CSX locomotives positioned, nose-to-nose. Then, the chief executive officers of each company, hard hats and all, joining hands in a victory salute. Once again, Associated Press PhotoWire carried the story and hundreds of newspapers used it.

photo by Ed Lallo

Remember that the news media loves good photos. Unusual subjects, action, the unexpected, people doing crazy things. "Eye candy" is what some news photographers and editors call great pictures. You see them all the time in *People* magazine, photos taken by skilled photographers who are always looking for appealing and clever angles to tell the story.

Not everyone can hire a professional photojournalist to help promote an event. But there is another option. Today, digital cameras have opened up new opportunities in media relations for all the rest of us.

With the availability of affordable digital cameras, we can take "newspaper-quality" photos of nearly any occasion. Pictures taken by amateurs and photography enthusiasts are used all the time by the news media.

But, remember: Always shoot the highest resolution photos you can if you believe they might be used by the news media. This simple technical consideration can make all the difference. The picture resolution of most digital cameras can be manually adjusted though either the Menu or Function settings. You will need to play around with it to find the highest resolution for your particular camera brand and model.

The optimum setting to get best quality is high resolution, low compression. That means you will get the maximum resolution on your camera with the least amount of compression, which might adversely affect quality.

When you choose these settings, you will note that the number of photos you can take on a particular memory card will decrease. That is because high-resolution photos require more space on a memory card.

You can get many more low-resolution photos on a memory card because each picture is smaller in size and the quality is not as good. I would only consider shooting low-resolution photos on my digital camera if the sole purpose were for use online. But, then, what would happen if I were to snap a picture-of-a-lifetime in low resolution? Sure, I could put it online but I could never use it in a publication—even 4 x 6 prints probably would look fuzzy.

It is always best to take high-resolution photos with a digital camera. Incidentally, you can solve everything by purchasing a larger capacity memory card and keeping your digital camera set at the highest resolution all the time. Now, you are ready to capture your own "eye-candy" photos.

Let's say you are doing media relations for an event. You have put together a list of media and drafted a news release in advance. Then, the day of the event arrives, and you get lucky by taking a digital picture that tells the whole story, a "WOW!" type of picture that people will rave about.

What you may have is something potentially more valuable for promoting your event than a news release or anything else. A great picture creates a lasting impression and is often preferred by editors rather than a news release to tell the story. All you need is a photo caption, a witty two or three lines that sum up the story that the picture tells. Then, get it into the hands of the media.

Remember, as with what happened at Learjet, one picture can change everything.

The Payoff of a Deskside Briefing

A deskside briefing with a reporter can be one of the best ways to generate initial interest about your company or organization. It's particularly effective because the tactic is not widely used by many public relations practitioners. If you play your cards right and if some basic rules are followed, the deskside session can lead to a good story.

The dynamic is to schedule an informal meeting with a reporter, get an understanding of the reporter's needs and talk briefly about your organization or issue. The objective of a deskside is to lay groundwork for a possible future story, guide editorial direction and build a relationship. It is not to pitch a story.

Let's say that a few journalists have written about your company, product or service but it would be a major coup to have a story appear in the *Daily Bugle* (yes, I'm making up that name).

Despite numerous calls to the person you think is the correct reporter at the *Bugle*, your calls are either not being returned or the reporter has told you that while the story seems interesting, what's lacking is a good news angle. That's a polite way for a reporter to tell you that he or she perceives your outfit as no big deal and not worthy of his or her time.

The more obvious and predictable approach of pitching a story, perhaps to a reporter you've never before met, has not worked. So, you need to try something else. You are under pressure to make something happen with the *Daily Bugle*. It's time for a…(drum roll, please)…*deskside briefing*. Here's how it works.

The concept is to get your CEO or an executive or an expert or you before the right reporter for a brief, early morning background meeting. The "deskside" is *not* billed as an interview but as a quick background briefing. Ideally, you should meet the reporter informally for about 30 minutes before his or her normal work starting time, and—this is very important—keep the meeting to less than the time you requested.

Before you make any phone calls to a newsroom, do some research about the reporter you are approaching to make certain you are calling the right one. Take a look at some of the recent things he or she has written so you can mention it in your conversation and compliment their work. Look for areas of overlap or connection between what they have previously written and your potential story.

All reporters have a particular "beat," often defined by their personal interests. NBC's Robert Hager, for example, has covered transportation issues for years because of his interest in aviation. Thomas Friedman at the *New York Times* has become one of the country's foremost opinion-leaders on the Middle East because of his interest in the region.

Sometimes, the way you find just the right reporter who is interested in your potential story will surprise you.

Several years ago, my marketing communications agency represented the World Cycling Championships, the annual series of bicycle races that had traditionally been held in Europe, mostly in Italy. The event was going to happen for the first time ever in the United States. No one had ever heard of it here, and our challenge was to boost advance awareness to help drive ticket sales and attendance.

Our strategy was to first develop a number of stories in major daily newspapers about the significance of the World Cycling Championships coming to America. Those newspapers stories would help to quickly build credibility for our story and attract television news coverage, because TV news decision-makers traditionally want to see a story "validated" in print first, before they invest the resources in covering it.

Right at the top of our list was the *Washington Post*. But we couldn't find a reporter at the *Post's* sports department who had any interest in cycling. You could talk all day with them about baseball, football and golf, but not about racing bicycles.

After doing some research, we found that a general assignment reporter assigned to the paper's Metro section had written a couple of stories about local bike races in the nation's capital because he was an avid cyclist himself. In fact, he rode his bicycle to work.

We called the reporter and suggested a briefing about the event. He agreed to meet us at the paper early one morning, about 45 minutes before normal starting time. That meeting resulted in not only one terrific story but continuing coverage of the event. We never asked him for a story, we just suggested a background briefing about our event.

Being concise is key when it comes to asking a journalist to meet. Create a brief, focused, alluring and—most of all—low-key pitch in order to schedule the meeting. Once you've got the right journalist, you need to "hook" their interest, the quicker the better. Your chances diminish the more you talk. Whether you leave a message on voicemail or actually get the reporter on the phone *live*, get right to the point with an action plan—tell them that you have a possible story in mind and why you think they might be interested, briefly referencing something similar that you have seen they have written.

When you have the right reporter on the phone, don't waste their time with trivial politeness unless you are personal pals. Avoid beginning the call with "How are you today?" Get right to the point.

And then, do something unusual—Do not pitch a story. That's too predictable. Say something like, "This may or may not lead to a story but I think it is important to at least give you a *brief* backgrounder about our organization and here's why...."

You are not pitching a story but merely seeking a meeting to provide background. This unique approach implies exclusiveness. It merits a reporter meeting you and your boss before work to at least listen. Underscore to the reporter that you know the importance of their work demands and, besides, your boss has a limited amount of time as well, so an early morning meeting would work best. Remember, it's an informal meeting.

Here are some general rules:

- It is best not to send information in advance of the deskside for a couple of reasons—first, it begins to feel like a predictable story pitch; second, you may be sending the wrong material; and third, the reporter is likely to lose or misplace the stuff sent in advance, which could create an awkward moment when you arrive and the reporter can't find it. Do not send advance material unless the reporter specifically insists on it, and then only send what they request, nothing more.

- Resist the traditional public relations urge to impress the reporter with reams of news media kits and "stuff." When you go to a deskside, intentionally take only the briefest supporting material with you. Preferably, no brochures, no media kit. I suggest taking only a one-page bio on the official who is meeting with the reporter. In that way, you create an opportunity to have personalized follow-up contact with the reporter by providing specific material the reporter wants as a result of the meeting. That not only keeps the reporter focused on your potential story, it also works to build a relationship of trust and confidence with the reporter and boosts your chances that a story will happen.

- Make sure, in advance, that your boss understands the purpose of the deskside briefing, especially that (1) it is not an interview but a briefing and (2) you are not asking the reporter to do a story. It's an informal chance to meet—for the first time—a journalist who can be important to your organization. It is *relationship-building*.

- During the meeting, focus on one or two main messages. Avoid making the reporter's eyes glaze over by talking about too many issues. Focus on a couple of competitive advantages that may match up with what the reporter has written about in the past.

- At the conclusion of a deskside briefing, define an informal follow-up plan. Ask the reporter if there is any material you can send that might be helpful. Find out how best you can stay in touch—e-mail, phone.

- Thank the reporter for his or her time. Show sincere appreciation. And do not—ever—ask for a story. Even if the reporter suggests a possible story, say you would be happy if the conversation led to that but you just appreciated chatting with them for a few minutes.

Once I took a CEO for an early morning deskside briefing with a reporter and, when the meeting concluded, the executive could not resist the urge, even though I had advised him against it, to ask, "When are you going to do a story?" The reporter understandably looked ambushed. The deskside meeting had been scheduled with the understanding that it was neither an interview nor an implied commitment to do a story. It was a unique opportunity to meet with a reporter who had or might have otherwise said "no" to a traditional interview. We had broken the ground rules of the meeting. It was like breaking a promise.

On the other hand, there are more stories about the effectiveness of deskside briefings. Newspaper columnist and talk show host Greg Dobbs tells of meeting with a public relations representative about the trend toward "just in time" manufacturing, a process to more efficiently manage often-costly inventories and make products more competitively priced.

"She made me aware of a concept growing in popularity in American industry," Dobbs says. "When she had my attention, she then offered her client to serve as my example in a feature story. It worked. Win-Win."

"She turned me on to the concept, and then, by getting me in her client's door, earned her pay."

A deskside briefing is a resourceful way to get before an important reporter and establish a productive working relationship that will pay off and, hopefully, help you get an edge on your competitors.

A Time and a Place for News Releases

News releases are, unfortunately, an overused crutch in the public relations business. Many public relations people criticize the news media for not paying attention to their organizations but rely solely on issuing a never-ending string of poorly written news releases that seldom have any relevance or news value and are often self-serving drivel.

Brian Lamb, the founder and chief executive officer of C-SPAN, says news releases are the worst way to communicate with the media. "Public relations people," he says, "simply do not understand that the media is certainly not driven by and generally does not care about news releases."

While a news release (not to be confused with "press" release, a phrase that went out of style with hula hoops) unquestionably can get the attention of a reporter or editor, it's not often that a release by itself results in a news story, except with smaller newspapers.

From a journalist's perspective, it's fairly rare to see a news release that contains legitimate, balanced news.

Yet, many public relations people—and their bosses—think that all they need to do is issue a release and the media will come running. It doesn't work that way.

Veteran journalists generally have become wary of trivial fluff or blatantly commercial self-promotion under the "news release" banner.

"When I get a news release telling me of a new hire, or burying the lead of a plausible story," says Denver-based newspaper columnist and talk show host Greg Dobbs, "then anything else I get from them feels like too much. Knowing my priorities means, among other things, knowing when I might use their information and knowing when I might not...which is 'when' they shouldn't send it in the first place."

Effective news releases must be just that—"news." Not fluff, not a sales promotion, certainly not "about" your company—but legitimate news. The news release must be…a story.

Here is just the lead paragraph of a classic example of "fluff," jargon-laden corporate promotion. Incidentally, I have changed the names of the two companies and the spokesperson but left in the one company's unnecessary use of the registered trademark (®) symbol:

> McLean, Va., January 10, 2005—ABC® Incorporated (NASDAQ: ABCD), a leading worldwide provider of business intelligence software, today announced that XYZ, Inc. has placed it in the visionary quadrant of both the Enterprise Business Intelligence Suites (EBIS) and BI Platform segments of XYZ Inc.'s 2004 "Magic Quadrants for Business Intelligence" report.

> "We are honored to be positioned so prominently in both the EBIS and BI Platforms Magic Quadrants," said ABC's COO Joe Smith. "We believe inclusion in both business intelligence quadrants highlights ABC's exceptional ability to support a complete spectrum of business users and a wide variety of reporting and analysis applications from a single, integrated architecture."

What's a "visionary quadrant" and what makes it "magic" and why is the news release written seemingly in jargon and code? Not only are terms not explained anywhere in the news release, but by the third paragraph, ABC® company has moved on to blatantly promote two new, completely unrelated products, never returning to explain why anyone on the planet should care about a "visionary quadrant" or "BI Platform."

Credibility is damaged when a company unabashedly uses an alleged news release as an advertisement. In this case, ABC company appeared to have used some fluffy excuse of a news release to promote its wares rather than buy an ad.

On the other hand, Nike, Inc. defused potentially adverse news of a store closing through a timely and comprehensively written news release that appeared to candidly present the full story. The headline read "Nike, Inc. to Cease Operations at NikeTown Orange County."

Beaverton, Ore. (3 January, 2005)—Today Nike, Inc. announces its plans to cease operations at NikeTown Orange County on January 30th, 2005. Opened in 1993, the store at Triangle Square Mall in Orange County was one of the first NikeTowns—the company's premiere retail space for showcasing innovative products and deepening Nike's connection to consumers. In recent years, however, the mall has experienced low tenant occupancy. As such, Nike believes that the closure of the store is in the best interest of the brand. We will continue to serve Orange County consumers through NikeTown Los Angeles, NikeWomen stores in Orange County (Newport Beach and Costa Mesa), nike.com and existing partners at retail.

Nike will support affected employees by offering all store associates competitive severance packages, in accordance with our guidelines and California labor laws. In addition, we encourage individuals to identify opportunities that fit their experience within the Company and apply accordingly.

This news release is professionally written and reflects a major company that wants to protect its brand while supporting customers and doing something for employees who will lose jobs. Nike, in laying out the situation with the store closing, subtly lays the problem on a shopping mall that may have some problems. The company also manages to include some cross-promotion in a classy manner.

News releases need a purpose, like the Nike example. What are you announcing and why is it important? Stick to one purpose and seek to establish credibility through candor and openness.

The general idea is to use the release not to provide the whole story but to capture the media's interest and make them want to learn more about the subject or issue. How do you achieve that?

Here are some ways:

- Take a journalist's perspective. Is your news release actually timely news that the media might find interesting or is it self-serving fluff? Develop a legitimate news story in the news release, something the media will find appealing.

- Cut to the chase. Why should anyone care? Get to the bottom line in the first sentence and then provide background in the body of the release. Isn't that how news stories are crafted by the media? They write a headline that catches your eye and then provide enough in the first sentence or two to whet your appetite. If you want to know more, read on…

- Be timely. This is one essential element of "news." Develop timely news releases.

- Keep the news release to one (1) page. You heard me…one page. I assure you that when you go beyond one page, the media's attention drops exponentially, regardless of what you have to say.

- Give the media an easy way to contact you and learn more—give 'em your phone numbers and make sure you answer and that it doesn't go to voicemail.

When developing a news release, remember that most releases are rarely if ever used, so be realistic and imaginative. Use news releases as working tools for journalists, to provide clarity on your messages and focus for what you have to say. Good news releases can be valuable weapons in the communications arsenal.

Most of all, don't oversell. A news release is supposed to showcase credible news that you have to announce—clear, compelling and straightforward. Avoid all those overworked promotion words—they don't work in a news release except to undermine your purpose and turn off reporters.

Paper the news media too many times with promotion or sales pieces under the guise of a "news release," and you will not only kill their interest in your organization when you have something real to announce, you will drive them to your competitor.

A news release recently crossed my desk from a chain of stores called "RETAIL♦MART." (I have changed the real name of the company for this example.) The one-page release contained the use of the company's logo—"RETAIL♦MART"—14 times, exactly like that. Not RetailMart or Retail Mart or even RETAILMART, but RETAIL♦MART. Such commercial branding not only does not belong in a news release but it hurts the credibility of the company because the news media most likely will disregard it.

And the enormous volume of releases with trivial subject matter can have the same adverse effect. A few years ago, the corporate communications department at Sprint—the long distance company—would issue a news release about every new hire at corporate headquarters at Overland Park, Kansas. There was no plan and certainly no strategic objective, just a bad habit. Some thought it was because the head of corporate communications at the time had limited experience in public relations.

The avalanche of daily news releases completely got out of hand and inundated BusinessWire, the paid news release distribution wire. Even though BusinessWire was making a bundle on all the Sprint business, the trivial nature of the releases was undermining credibility for both Sprint and BusinessWire to the point that the wire service sent a representative to Sprint headquarters to politely ask them to get a grip.

Sprint is certainly not the only company that has cranked out meaningless news releases. The practice is more often the case than the exception. Yet, the news media is not driven by and generally doesn't care about news releases, to echo the words of C-SPAN's Brian Lamb.

Effective media relations is about having solid contacts among journalists and knowing how to present a story idea.

"I find that 90 percent of PR people do a really poor job," says Barbara Bradley Hagerty of National Public Radio. "They pitch stories with no angles, just kind of pitch randomly. They don't think through that journalists need a *news* peg. They don't offer specifics for sources to back up the story or how we can cover it quickly."

"Rarely is a story pitched right," according to Richard Danbury of BBC Television News in London. "I suppose a key here is to know the journalists' preoccupations and pitch accordingly. When I was a lawyer, I was taught the golden rule of advocacy: know thy tribunal."

If You Write a News Release,
Write an Effective One!

Despite the potential shortcomings mentioned in the last chapter, writing a news release can be one of the biggest opportunities in media relations. It's all in how you do it. To fully take advantage of that opportunity, you must make a news release *news*. Make it a real, legitimate news story. Each day, the news media is bombarded with thousands of trivial, self-serving news releases. So, imagine your competitive edge if you create a news release that contains genuine news!

All kinds of events can provide the opportunity for a good news release. A release can announce a new product or service, react to a timely situation, trumpet a new development at your organization, provide perspective about an event, or attempt to present your side in an adverse situation.

Even such a generally mundane news release as one that announces a new hire or promotion within your organization can be meaningful if you consider how the hire or promotion enhances value or provides service to your key audiences. A new-hire news release might read something like this: "As XYZ Company increases emphasis on customer service, the company announces that Mary Smith has accepted the position of vice president of customer satisfaction...."

To help you focus on its news content, imagine how your news release might appear if it were run verbatim in the newspaper as actual news. (In real life, of course, that rarely happens—although some PR people claim otherwise).

Here are examples of four basic types of news release, although the lines between them sometimes blur:

- Announcement. This is a common kind of news release used to announce such events as new products or services; new employees; promotions; reports about sales, earnings, mergers and financials; openings and closings; expansion and construction of facilities; lay-offs and employment opportunities.

- Spot or Timely Announcement. This type of news release often announces an upcoming event or occurrence. It can be driven by outside occurrences over which you may have no control, such as a natural disaster, inclement weather or terrorism. A spot announcement is used to provide timely information updates to the news media.

- Controlled Message Announcement. This is the type of news release organizations use to try to suppress bad news and get across their message in an adverse environment. This kind of news release usually makes matters worse because an organization is perceived (often accurately) as hiding behind the release rather than engaging in a healthy interaction with the news media.

- Reaction Release. A reaction news release is generally used in a time-critical situation when it is important to comment on something that affects an organization, such as new legislation or a lawsuit. It is also used to provide an organization's position on some timely outside occurrence that has some bearing on the organization. For example, if a federal agency has announced new guidelines for the industry in which your company does business, a reaction release can help position your organization as a leader.

So, get in a news frame of mind. Sit down and actually *read* today's newspaper. Look at how headlines are written and pay special attention to how the first paragraph or two of each story is written. You want to clone that style of writing in a news release.

Next, plan your news release. Here are some steps to follow each and every time you have a news release to draft. First, ask yourself these questions:

- What's the purpose? Why are you doing a news release? In many cases, it's because the boss thought it was a good idea or the "suits" in the front office cooked up some new sales promotion, and they're hoping a news release will get them results without the expense of buying ads. If your reasons fit into those categories, that's not good enough. Sure, a news release can legitimately and credibly announce a new sales promotion but it can never drive sales. You need to establish a clear and focused purpose for the news release.

- Is your news "newsworthy"? The purpose of a news release is to inform a public audience through the news media of your news item. Do not use your news release to try and make a sale. A good news release answers all of the "W" questions (who, what, where, when and why), providing the media with useful information about your organization, product, service or event. If you read your news release and it reads like an advertisement, rewrite it.

- Who is it designed to reach and why should they care? A news release is not a place to dance around getting to the point. Your message goes hand-in-hand with the purpose, and you must get to the point right away. Vaguely defined news releases, lacking purpose, are one of the biggest irritants to journalists who receive them. There might be actual news hidden in there somewhere but it takes too long to find. Remember that most news releases are reviewed for nanoseconds in a newsroom due to the volume received every day.

- What is in it for this particular audience? What are the potential values or the benefits or rewards to a public audience? Again, consider these factors from an outsider's perspective.

- What is the goal of your organization in issuing a news release? Is there a call-to-action? A timely event that you want people to attend? A new product hitting the market that will make life easier?

Some other points to remember:

- Be timely. One of the best ways to get the media to pay attention to your news release is to make it timely. You can get a reporter's attention by providing the scoop on a news story that's about to happen. You can enhance the appeal, if possible, by explaining how your news release is relevant to other timely and important news. For example, if you are announcing a "healthy lifestyles" fair at a local shopping mall in a news release and you notice that there have been a number of stories on television and in the newspapers about obesity, look for a way to position your event as a solution to a problem.

- Write for the news media. Journalists will commonly use a news release as a springboard for a larger feature story. Try to develop a story as you would like to have it told. Even if your news is not reprinted verbatim, it may provide an acceptable amount of exposure.

- Stick to the facts. Tell the truth. Avoid fluff, embellishments and exaggerations. If you feel that your news release contains embellishments perhaps it would be a good idea to set it aside until you have more exciting news to share. If you get outside the facts, remember you might be risking your organization's credibility, reputation and brand. It never hurts to tone it down a bit.

- Use an active voice. A passive voice is bland. Verbs in the active voice help to bring your news release to life.

- Use the present tense. Avoid writing that "the company announced." Instead, say that "the company announces" or "is announcing."

- Beware of jargon. While a limited amount of jargon will be required if your goal is to optimize your news release for online search engines, the best way to communicate your news is to speak plainly, using ordinary language. Jargon is language specific to certain professions or groups and is not appropriate for general readership. Avoid such terms as "capacity planning techniques," "extrapolate" and "prioritized evaluative procedures."

- Avoid hype. The exclamation point (!) will kill your credibility with the media.

A news release should be well written and follow a basic format. Good margins, double-spaced lines, short paragraphs and meaningful quotes make it easy to read.

Follow a standard format that can subtly help brand the image of your organization, although keep in mind that a news release is not an advertisement. A release should follow a style that makes it *look* like a story within a format that the media recognizes. Remember, a news release is like telling a story but you are getting to the point of the story in the first sentence.

Here are some formatting rules for news releases:

- Double space your text.
- Use a standard serif font, such as Times New Roman or Palatino Linotype, in 10 or 12 point type.
- Don't indent paragraphs and double-space between paragraphs.
- Number the pages.
- Write "more" at the end of each page if the release continues.
- Use the old journalistic symbol "###" at the end of your release.

Here is a summary of the elements of a news release, based on the Associated Press style for news releases preferred by most newspapers:

For Immediate Release. Underline it. Bold it, if you wish, and left justify it at the top of your page. That signals the media that you have something to say right now. Never ever use the phrase "Advance for Release." That was in style a decade or so ago and perceived by the media as manipulative. There's nothing to be gained by saying "Here's something so hot that you cannot use it now but I wanted to let you in on it early…."

Date. That's the day of the week and date of your release. For example "Tuesday, March 2, 2005." The day and date go right under For Immediate Release. Using both day and date is a good practice because despite all our best intentions, we sometimes make mistakes on dates alone. And there's an old jinx that says when you put just the date with no day, two times out of four, it'll be wrong. Go figure.

Headline. Write a headline for your news release that looks like one right out of *USA Today*. Make it catchy and seductive. For example, AARP created a promotion under the banner: "Gray & Glamorous: AARP's Golden Girls" about seven actresses, age 56 to over 70, who are considered among "Hollywood's hottest." It got them coverage everywhere, including *USA Today*.

Location. This is a city or place, for example:
(Columbus, OH) The lead sentence starts here...

The lead paragraph. The lead is the most important part of any news release. This is your best chance at capturing a journalist's attention. In just a couple of sentences, you must give the reader basic yet compelling details of the story. So, get right to the point of why anyone should care about your news or announcement. Keep the lead paragraph short—two to three short sentences maximum and no more than about four or five lines.

Body of text. This forms the apex of the journalistic "inverted pyramid" style of writing. What this means is that the first paragraph summarizes the most important part of the story. It gets to the "bottom line." The body of text contains several paragraphs that provide the details, including facts, supporting information and relevant quotes.

And by the way, it is okay to use your organization's letterhead. There's no compelling benefit in having a special "News Release" letterhead.

While it is nearly impossible and certainly not particularly smart to suggest a hard and fast set of rules for a news release, there are four basic paragraphs or components of an effective release. These components comprise the elements of the "inverted pyramid" approach to writing a news release:

Paragraph One—Most important facts of the release. This is the attention grabber.

Paragraph Two—Essential background material and the names of key characters or sources.

Paragraph Three—Elaboration on material contained in the first paragraph plus additional background information.

Paragraph Four—Concise summary of the news in the release.

Contact. At the end of the news release, include the contact person's full name, office and cell phone numbers and e-mail address. Here is an example:

> Contact: Beth Jones
> Office: (703) 555-1212
> Cell: (202) 555-2323
> E-mail: bjones63@msn.com

Ultimately, though, all the structure and format in the world won't save you without good content—what you have to say. Use the news release format to tell a timely and relevant story. A story that is compelling, interesting, informs, motivates and excites the news media to immediately form a good opinion of your organization. Use it as a door-opener, an entrée to journalists, to develop good coverage.

Media Lists—Less Is Better

There's a popular misconception in the public relations industry that the larger the media list—the more names on it—the better. During my public relations agency years, I've found this to be particularly characteristic of corporate communications departments in large companies. Quantity over quality is the conventional wisdom.

In fact, an entire cottage industry of service companies that offer media lists has sprung up. Thousands and thousands of names. The series of Bacon's (bacons.com) Media Directories, for example, has gotten so thick and heavy that it's hard just to lift the books onto your desk. Bacon's and other services, like Burrelle's Media Directory (burrelles.com), are also available online in a user-friendly and much lighter format.

Vocus (vocus.com) another one of the numerous online services that provide media relations support, boasts "access to a global media directory of over 400,000 unique journalists, updated daily." Holy cow! Am I impressed? Absolutely not.

Unquestionably, these services deliver specific contact information about people in the news media, but are all those names really needed by your organization? And are they worth the expense? The answer is, unquestionably, "No."

A "shotgun" approach to media relations seldom works and often tends to hurt your reputation rather than help it.

It's always important to maintain an up-to-date list of media contacts but quality of contacts is far more important than quantity. Many public relations people are insecure and concerned they might miss sending something to someone important in the news media, but it's not necessary to pepper a whole newsroom with your releases.

The news media are inundated every day by too much stuff that's too poorly targeted. In some cases, the same media materials are sent to multiple reporters and editors, regardless of whether they cover the issue or not. Some of it is sent to reporters at organizations where they haven't worked for years. Yet, in other cases, the right reporter doesn't receive a copy.

An important element of effective media relations is targeting the right journalists with a story angle that might capture their interest.

The single most valuable piece of advice offered by Scott Simon, host on National Public Radio, is, "Know who you are calling. I am amazed at the number of calls I get from people representing books (like "100 Ways to Grow a Great Rutabaga!"), CDs or people that no one who listens to our program should think we would be interested in. We don't keep our show a secret; several million people listen. Before you call us, you should try to put yourself among them, at least for a week or two, to make a better informed presentation."

So, how do you start crafting a media list that will achieve results?

Stop for a minute and think about the number of reporters who have written anything about your organization or business in the last year. You will generally find that this is no more than a handful.

Of course, if you work for a high profile company with many consumer products and services—such as Microsoft, Coca-Cola, GE or Colgate—it may be a different story. But even then, it is likely that only a few reporters will follow your outfit on a regular basis and do the substantive reporting that influences other journalists.

A few years ago, as senior vice president for the corporate image and reputation management practice at Edelman Public Relations, I encountered the head of communications for a major aerospace company who had never bothered, in two years on the job, to learn the name of one single reporter who covered his company. He told me, flatly, that he hired us to deal with the media because he didn't want to be bothered. Such an attitude is blatantly irresponsible, and it's not surprising that the fellow subsequently lost his job.

I'd be willing to bet that for most corporations, there are fewer than a dozen reporters who really count when it comes to getting out a story about the organization, and it is the job of the person in charge of media relations to establish and skillfully nurture relationships with these reporters.

And while you are making contacts among reporters and editors, don't overlook the wire services. The stories written by reporters at the Associated Press, Reuters and Bloomberg appear in hundreds of newspapers. Those reporters are the "media influencers." They set the tone for others, and they are critical to your organization. Find them and court them. Communicate with them personally on a regular basis, never through an intermediary service. Get to know them and what they need and seek in story ideas.

Here's a checklist for creating an effective "top tier" media list:

- Get online and find out who writes about your organization. Use an online news retrieval service, such as ProQuest or Nexis, to find all the original stories written about your organization in the last year. These archiving services provide access, usually with a nominal charge, to thousands of current periodicals and newspapers, many updated daily and containing full-text articles that date back to the mid-to-late 1980s. You want to find stories in which a reporter invested some time and wrote a substantial piece of journalism about your organization or business arena. Make a list of those reporters and pay particular attention to the ones who have written thoughtful pieces about your company. Put them at the top of the list.

- Invest in resource materials. If your budget will allow it, consider the services of a respected news media contact service, such as Bacon's or Burrelle's. They will provide the basic information about specific media, reporters, beats and contact information. But don't let them do your job for you. The news business is transient. Reporters move around a lot, either within their company or between other news organizations. Consequently, there's a chance that today's accurate media contact information will be outdated tomorrow.

- Make phone calls. Get the latest and most accurate media contact information. Reach out to news organizations that are important to you. If your online research hasn't turned up good results, no problem. Simply make a list of media that you believe might be interested in reporting your story or, more important, where you would like to see your story appear, and give them a call. Let's say, for example, that you work for a not-for-profit group that develops after school programs to help urban youth, and you want to generate media coverage in cities like Philadelphia, Boston and Atlanta. It's easy. Begin by calling the Metro or local news assignment desks of the local media in those cities. Ask who covers education or inner city issues and speak with that reporter. Most journalists are eager to know of an interesting new story. A phone call to a news organization often leads to the most valuable kind of contact. That's a key step in getting ready for a story pitch to the media.

- Test the water. If in doubt about whether you have a "news story," ask when you call a news organization to get updated contact details. There is nothing wrong with calling a reporter who you have identified as being interested in your organization and saying "I think I've got the elements of a good story for you but I need a little help giving it focus." You will be surprised as the helpful guidance you will receive.

- Keep it professional. Find out how they prefer to be contacted about future news from your business and get all their contact details. Remember, it's not a conversation. Effective media relations is a ritual. You have called the reporter to plant the seeds of initial interest and ask them how they wanted to be contacted about stories. Your goal is to present a story idea in such a seductive way as to elicit a response from the journalist to know more.

- Update. Even the most effective media lists don't last forever. Reporters change jobs and assignments. Make it a practice to update your entire media list at least every quarter. It's easy to do because of the contact information you've collected. If someone doesn't respond, give him a call. If there's still no response, assume there's been a change and call that department at the newspaper to make inquiries and gather fresh contact details. In my media relations consulting practice, in which I work with numerous reporters all the time, I will routinely get e-mails from journalists who are changing jobs or assignments.

"If there is one piece of advice I'd give PR people," says Jon Ashworth, business columnist with the *Times* of London, "it would be: 'Think before you ring.'"

"It's amazing how many people call up right on deadline with some inane query or story proposal. It doesn't take a genius to figure out that you don't ring a journalist between 4 p.m. and 7 p.m. other than in response to a story of the day. I find that 11 to 12 is a good time, since journalists are between the morning news meeting and lunch. Also, work out who you are calling: I work for the daily *Times* and get calls for the *Sunday Times*."

Effective relationships with the news media are not something to take casually or pass along to a third party, such as a public relations agency, unless you are absolutely assured that contacts will be professionally managed.

National Public Radio's Barbara Bradley Hagerty counsels PR professionals to "figure out who you should get in touch with and go to that person directly. Work with that right person as opposed to contacting everyone. That's annoying."

The best and most responsible media coverage is usually the result of developing an ongoing professional relationship with a journalist who is interested in your story.

Again, influential media relations is all about *relationships*, which engender trust, respect and integrity.

"The best public relations people," according to Richard Serrano, Washington correspondent for the *Los Angeles Times*, "are those who are honest and forthright with information, who are willing to steer you to the right aspect of a story without compromising their side. The worst are those who refuse to comment or cooperate, and end up actually hurting their client."

Remember, it doesn't require all that much time or expense to create and maintain a great media list because the most valuable list need not be lengthy but rather focused, accurate and updated regularly.

News/Talk Radio—You Gotta Love It!

News/talk radio stations, usually on the AM band, are popular from New York to Little Rock, Wilmington to Sacramento. There are hundreds of stations, many of them on the air 24 hours a day.

One of the most colorful of them is WQSV—AM 790 in Ashland City, Tennessee. Run by an equally colorful radio veteran named Corky Albright, the station is like something right out of *Northern Exposure,* a quirky television program of the late 1980s. The door is always open, and the microphone is always available to just about anyone in the community who has something to share. America needs more radio stations like WQSV.

News/talk radio is an excellent way of reaching wide audiences to talk about your organization and in a media environment where you can present a controlled message that gives people a better understanding. And talk radio stations have a lot of time on the air to fill and a big appetite for interview guests, especially if they are informative and entertaining. If you are a hit, chances are you will be asked to return.

Phil Knight, the founder of Nike, at first was a little reluctant when Edelman Public Relations booked him for an interview with Jim Bohannon, host of the Jim Bohannon Radio Show on Mutual and Westwood One Radio Networks, a few years ago. But when it was over, Knight said it was one of the best interview opportunities ever. Bohannon asked logical questions and Knight was allowed to talk about the dream he turned into a $12 billion athletic shoe and clothing company. Bohannon's program is carried live on over 300 stations nationwide.

Whether for an hour or three minutes, news/talk radio provides a forum for you to reach out and speak to new and existing audiences. Radio gives you the opportunity to casually mention the positioning message that differentiates your organization from competitors.

Okay, you are convinced that news/talk radio is a good media relations tactic. How do you begin to schedule interviews?

The online service NewsLink (newslink.org) provides one of the most comprehensive lists of news/talk radio stations in the United States. And a full listing of NPR stations is available at www.npr.org. Many NPR stations feature live interview programs, usually in the mid-morning.

As with creating a media list, it's important to do initial homework to identify the programs that might best showcase your interview subject.

The easiest way is to create a media spreadsheet that includes city, radio station, programs, names of producers and contact information. Keep in mind that some news/talk stations might run feature programs at one time of the day and sports talk programs at another time. A quick phone call to the station will help guide you to the right program. You will also be able to determine the general length of interview they prefer and whether they will interview guests by telephone or insist that guests be in their studio.

By the way, never call either the general manager or the station manager but rather ask to speak with a show producer. Deal with the people who get the programs on the air. They are the gatekeepers.

When you are satisfied with your list, begin making calls approximately one month before the time you hope to book the interview. NPR stations generally plan a month in advance. Some news/talk stations will only plan a couple of weeks out.

A big factor that will influence when an interview is scheduled is the timeliness of your interview. Is it tied to a holiday or event? Is it seasonal? Remember that the news media embraces timely news angles and interviews.

Make your bid for a radio interview concise and compelling. Once you identify the program you want to appear on, work to get the producer on the telephone, live. It may require a few calls.

Explain briefly what's special about the interview you propose and why it might be of interest to the show's audience. Suggest a possible date and, if possible, a reason for seeking that date. Remember, attempt to make it a timely interview subject, such as back-to-school, an anniversary, an event, a time of year or whatever. A timely angle will help convince a producer to book the interview.

Once you have a "yes" from the producer for an interview, suggest possible background material that you can provide. Keep it brief, such as a bio on the person to be interviewed, a one-page informative fact sheet and a list of possible questions. Avoid inundating a radio producer with material unless they ask for it.

The benefits of being interviewed on talk radio programs are significant. When the microphone is on, the door is open to say what you have to say, weave in marketing messages, deliver a compelling story and get a broad audience of listeners interested and excited and establish a favorable impression.

Be Clever but Not Too Clever

There was a public relations person I knew in Denver who felt that the only way to get the media's attention was to do something flashy. So, when sending out a news release, she would also fill the envelope with glittery confetti. You know, the metallic stuff that's impossible to vacuum up from a carpet. I suppose she didn't feel that the content of her releases could stand up alone so she wanted to make sure her mailings were noticed.

They were noticed all right—after making the mistake of opening her confetti-filled envelopes a couple of times, reporters and editors just pitched the whole thing, unopened, into the nearest trash can. Rather than becoming recognized as a credible public relations person, she developed a reputation as a prankster.

Everyone, including journalists, enjoys imaginative new ideas that get their attention. But if your idea only distracts the recipients, or annoys them by filling their carpets with confetti, you've lost the battle.

Unfortunately, in the public relations business, which should be distinguished by clever thinking, imaginative new ideas are few and far between. The business is instead driven by the same worn-out tactics over and over...and over.

There is nothing wrong with trying to get the media's attention through a small gift so long as it's relevant to the story and not something expensive or valuable that might compromise a journalist's integrity or get them in hot water with their company's rules about accepting gifts. (It's easy enough to find out what those rules are by making a few phone calls to reporters who cover your organization.)

Gifts to the media present a challenge that can rival the creative thought you invest in developing an imaginative story pitch and supporting background materials in the first place. I have seen some public relations agencies actually spend more time trying to figure out what gifts to get than on the messages and image they hope to see in print. In the end, too many such gifts are a waste of time and money.

On one occasion, while I was visiting a local television news producer, he sardonically asked if I needed any "oil rags" for my car. At first, I wasn't sure what he meant until he pointed to a pile of T-shirts, all with a promotional message for this or that event or product. They'd been sent along with media kits and news releases by PR people. What struck me was that all the T-shirts were white and emblazoned in HUGE print in the cheapest sort of way. Certainly, they were not something anyone would wear.

My friend, the producer, commented that some people in the newsroom jokingly maintained hope that someday, a really nice T-shirt might arrive that someone might not be embarrassed to wear—but hopes were fading. What was happening is the reverse of good media relations—the arrival each day of more and more white T-shirts eroded more and more of the news staff's confidence in the credibility of the senders. The message was lost.

Some public relations person's "clever idea" of capturing the media's attention by sending a T-shirt along with the news release was backfiring.

PR stunts are also fraught with hazard. There was an infamous incident in the mid-1990s when cardboard boxes with air holes in them started turning up at newspaper offices all over London. The journalists to whom they were addressed opened them to find live pigeons inside—a PR stunt designed to draw attention to a new investment product. The parcel came with instructions to release the pigeons outside.

The stunt backfired spectacularly—the animal rights lobby went on the warpath—and the PR agency that cooked up the stunt lost the account.

The technology industry has been among the most ineffective in handling media relations, largely because of the limited scope of experience and creativity among the young people doing PR in that business. Despite all the useful new ideas in technology, the industry as a whole does a pretty unimaginative job when it comes to promoting itself, most often copying some old idea or something a competitor is trying.

Not only is the tech industry T-shirt crazy but if I've seen one "stress ball" or coffee mug imprinted with the name of a tech outfit, I've seen a hundred of them.

MicroStrategy, once a technology high-flyer and known for giving out stress balls and coffee mugs, tried a little different approach and handed out samples of their information technology product on a compact disc for reporters. When inserted into a computer, however, the CD caused the computer to crash and resulted in corrupted files and damage that required hours to correct. Imagine the aggravation to a reporter who relied on the computer to finish a story. A marketing person at MicroStrategy apologetically said that there had been a "glitch" in the software for the media. No kidding.

Speaking of quality, Subaru, the Japanese car maker, once gave reporters clever-looking rollerball pens. Heck, every reporter needs another writing instrument. Problem was the pens would bulge up and leak ink under the normal pressure of a commercial airliner.

More than just a bad idea in media relations, few of these "trash-and-trinket" approaches have any relevance to the message a company or organization is promoting. For the media, which sees and experiences story bombardments from all directions, these approaches often only further erode credibility. Such stuff is generally thrown away, along with the "press" kits.

There are people, however, who I would consider Masters of the Universe when it comes to stunts and "stuff" that captures valuable and influential media attention.

Many reporters in New York still remember Sir Richard Branson arriving in Times Square atop an Army tank to promote his new Virgin Cola—an event that happened years ago! The tank signified challenging the competition and moving into new territory. Guess where the photo event took place? Right in front of Branson's Virgin Record store in Manhattan. Talk about brilliant cross-promoting of a brand!

Everything the Virgin Group used to promote the event was relevant to the occasion. Everything was first-class. The event was bold almost to the point of being outrageous (but of course, this was in New York, right?!).

Yet the message was understated to reflect the class and quality of Branson's product. It all worked together.

When I was head of corporate communications at Gulfstream Aerospace, we always challenged the relevance of promotional materials to the news media. We never distracted from the message in anything, such as a news release, by sending anything else with it.

But we had a promotional tool that no one else on earth had—an ultra long-range Gulfstream V business jet that could fly higher—50,000 feet—and farther—6,500 nautical miles—than most other aircraft in service.

In working with the news media, the only rule we had was that the reporter needed to write at least part of his or her story while at 50,000 feet, up above all other aircraft traffic, where the sky is nearly cobalt blue and you can clearly see the curvature of the earth.

When I took the first Gulfstream V aircraft on a world demo tour, we kept it simple by giving each reporter who flew with us up to 50,000 feet a top-quality pilot's flight cap, embroidered "Gulfstream V—World Tour." Was it an imaginative idea? Well, I've seen better. Was it relative to the event? You bet! Only those people who flew on the aircraft got a cap. I know of some journalists who, years later, still covet those hats because they can still boast of flying in a GV to an altitude of 50,000, nearly the edge of space. It was simple and classy and relevant.

There's nothing wrong with using "trash and trinkets" to drive home a promotional message as long as the campaign is imaginative, savvy and, most of all, relevant to the story. If it distracts, forget it.

The Media Pitch

You have compiled a strong list of media contacts and drafted some background materials. Now it's time to make the first call to pitch your story. It's time to be imaginative and quick-witted. But what do you say? Where to begin?

Because there are more possible options and variables in presenting a story to the news media than there are colors in the rainbow, it's probably best to just listen to what journalists say.

"The phase 'this would be perfect for you' is one to make me wary," says National Public Radio's Scott Simon.

Lisa Guernsey at the *New York Times* says that the best PR people have already done their homework before calling her, and they know what she is looking for in a story.

"They seem to know what might interest me, they are creative about offering story ideas, they understand that I write about trends more than companies, and they are willing to let an idea drop if I show no interest," Guernsey says.

On the other hand, Guernsey says a PR person is wasting her time about a story that has recently appeared in the *Times* or is nowhere near her field of interest. That's an annoyance, she says.

"Sometimes, people will hear you do one interview with a mushroom farmer and assume, somehow, that you have become a program for mushroom farmers," says NPR's Simon. "We will be flooded with pitches to interview mushroom farmers who are more witty, thoughtful or interesting than the one we have already had on.

"PR people should know: Because we do a mushroom farmer one week, we will probably not want to do another for some time to come."

Jim Bohannon, talk show host on Mutual and Westwood One Radio Networks, counsels media relations people to be selective in what they pitch and to whom and to be clear in explaining why his audience should care about it.

"I've been badgered by a few PR people with follow-up calls even though I said 'No.' I know some clients are really important, and you can get desperate. But we won't forget who clung to our ankles," Bohannon says.

A CNN producer reminds us that journalists will remember who is good at media relations and who isn't.

Sandra Pinkard, who produces The Diane Rehm Show on National Public Radio, says "most PR people I hear from are quick, to the point and respectful of my time. I also really appreciate the help I get from some in-house public relations people during off-hours, such as over weekends."

A reporter at the *Miami Herald* suggests: "Be candid with reporters when pitching a story idea; don't oversell or hype a story because it just hurts your credibility. Too often I have found PR people pitching their best-case scenario version, or the angle they want written, but that version falls apart once the reporting starts. And that puts a cloud over the whole thing.

"If you don't know, or won't really be able to give access, lay it out. There's nothing worse than starting to report something along certain contours offered by a public relations professional then realizing that the pitch was wrong, or manipulative or just plain ignorant."

When pitching a story to a television news program, remember that there are big differences in style between network and local news. Television news is all about *visuals—visuals—visuals*.

A producer for the ABC World News Tonight points out that most public relations people "do not have a solid understanding of what kind of stories producers at national networks—versus local stations—can get on their programs. Many PR people also seem unprepared to answer basic questions about visuals involved in their pitch—obviously an essential piece of any story for television."

She goes on to say "it can be frustrating when PR people only seem to know the two- or three-sentence "headline" of a story but cannot answer more in-depth questions that come up in initial conversations. We producers love getting good story ideas and are more open to pitch them to our superiors if we, ourselves, can get a solid and quick handle on what the story is all about."

Nora Dennehy, a television producer at BBC News, says public relations people "need to have a peg for a particular story and then need to be able to supply or point us in the direction of good case studies or experts for their particular story and for television they need to understand that we always must have pictures to illustrate a particular point."

Timing can be everything in landing good media coverage of your story. Broadcast producer and journalist Pat Piper says, "Anticipate. Know when a congressional committee is going to schedule a hearing, and get out there ahead of it. Know when an anniversary of some sort is coming, and get out in front of it."

Another piece of advice: Don't play favorites. Washington-based newspaperman Lyle Denniston says "nothing so infuriates a journalist working for a respectable news organization as to discover that a PR organization is serving media organizations differently, giving special favor and attention to a few. You will recognize this as the resentment of PR catering to Big Foot news organizations.

"I am always baffled, in fact, to discover that a PR organization intent on reaching a wide segment of the public is willing to treat some news organization's readers or listeners as if they were second-class, simply because they are getting news from someone other than a Big Foot. Medium or small news outlets do not need flattery, but neither do they need to be ignored."

And be realistic. Pat Piper tells of his worst experience with a media relations person, while producing The Larry King Show. "A PR lady called to say she had a Russian TV anchorwoman—the Russian version of Paula Zahn. I said 'yes' to an interview. The anchor lady shows up at the studio and can't speak English." The public relations person never mentioned that little detail.

The best people in media relations, according to Richard Serrano of the *Los Angeles Times*, "are those who are honest and forthright with information, willing to steer you to the right aspect of a story without compromising their side. The worst are those who refuse to comment or cooperate and end up actually hurting their client or organization."

Lisa Guernsey at the *New York Times* sums it up by saying, "public relations people can be extremely helpful, and the ones who impress me most are those who admit their limitations up front."

Effective media relations today is built on a foundation of respect, trust and a working relationship with reporters who have an interest in your organization and your story. It requires a discipline, a learning of what the media needs for a news story, keeping up to date on what specific reporters are writing and a healthy dose of good timing.

Before you even pick up the phone, make sure you have done your homework. Match the story of your media pitch with the right journalist. Be concise in what you say. Explain the potential importance or relevance of your story idea to the reporter's audience. If there are several sides to the story, build your own credibility (and that of your organization) by providing a brief but comprehensive perspective, including the "other side's" point of view. Offer background details, facts and statistics. Suggest how the story might be supported by visuals or photos. Most of all, get to the point and don't be long-winded.

By being attuned to how media relations works from a journalist's perspective, an organization can enjoy accurate news coverage that is credible and influential toward achieving whatever goals you establish or can imagine.

The Interview

Much of this book has focused on media relations from a journalist's perspective—understanding how journalists approach their jobs and what elements need to come together to create legitimate "news." Having this understanding about the workings of the news media can give you a competitive edge and help prepare you to speak with the media.

An interview with the news media can occur at any time and any place. An interview can be planned or occur spontaneously, without warning. An interview may result because you have called a contact at the local newspaper with a good, timely story about your organization. Or, the telephone rings and a reporter at the other end of the line is asking for just a few minutes of your time to answer some questions.

Either way, the primary objective of effective media relations is to communicate the story you want to tell as clearly and accurately as possible in a managed and controlled way that will help ensure that good things are written about you or your organization. The job of a reporter is to ferret out a story that will be of interest to readers, listeners or viewers.

An interview is not a conversation. It is a ritual in which the reporter seeks a news story, sometimes based on a preconceived notion, and you want to deliver focused messages that credibly tell your story. You want good coverage, the reporter just wants news. Remember, it's not a conversation.

Here's a list of "dos" and "don'ts" about interviews that I have learned from many years as a network news correspondent and then as a marketing communications agency executive.

First, the things you can do in an interview:

Always remember, it's your agenda. You do an interview not to help out a reporter but to communicate a positive message or image about your organization. Set your own boundaries. If a reporter calls out of the blue for an interview, you are under no obligation to drop everything and give an interview at that moment. Explain that you are finishing up something and will call the reporter back in 30 minutes. Ask about the subject he or she wants to discuss. Never ask for a list of specific questions because this compromises the working ethics of journalism and you will start off on the wrong foot. Then, take that 30 minutes or so to focus on what you want to say and communicate in the interview. This time will also help settle nerves that many people experience when contacted by the news media.

Always think three. Think of three messages you want to communicate in the interview. Think of how to deliver each message in an interesting and concise way. This is the core of what you want to communicate in the interview so be prepared to stick with these messages. Memorize them. By having three messages, you can enhance control of an interview by providing depth and perspective. One message is emotional in nature, such as a shared human experience. One message is logical; "it only makes sense." And one message is analytical, backing up your other messages with facts and data. Three messages—emotional, logical and analytical—working together present your side in the most compelling and controllable manner possible. It's a tactic that boosts your chances of controlling the interview and landing a good story.

Always seek opportunities to "bridge" to your three points. A "bridge" is an interview tactic to control and redirect an interview. If the reporter asks a question, for example, that is far afield from what you want to talk about, no problem. Acknowledge him by answering the question, briefly, then "bridge" back to your messages. A "bridge" can be just a few words, such as "I believe one of the most important things to remember is…" or "We need to keep in mind that…." And then, get back on track with your messages. Remember, it's your interview so make the most of it.

I recall once, as a young reporter in Washington, DC, watching Sen. Edward Kennedy being interviewed by a gaggle of reporters in a hallway of the United States Capitol building. I remember being in awe of the poise and skills that allowed him, despite having questions thrown at him from all directions, to stay focused on precisely what he wanted to say. I imagined that if I were to say something like, "Excuse me, Senator, your fly is open!" he would not even look down but would instinctively use a bridge phrase, like "yes, I know," and transition immediately back to his message. Of course, I didn't really say anything like that.

Always anticipate all questions. When you know in advance that a reporter is doing an interview, you can do a little online research on other stories the reporter has written and can get a good feel for what questions will be asked. Never go into an interview without first making a list of questions, even tough questions, you believe a reporter might ask. Ask colleagues to join in this exercise. It's a good way to quickly rehearse what you might say in an interview. If you "wing it," you are headed for trouble and may lose any chance for control of the interview and the outcome you desire.

Always know when to stop. The shorter the answer, the better. The best answer to a reporter's question is a concise answer. I cannot tell you the hundreds of times I have heard a reporter ask a question that deserves just a 30-second response but receives a five-minute answer that makes the reporter's eyes glaze over. It's like asking someone what time it is, and they build you a clock. As a general rule, keep answers to 30 seconds or less during a broadcast interview and a minute or less in an interview with the print media. If a reporter thinks a certain answer is too short, she can always ask a follow-up question.

Always answer the question you were asked. Listen to each question. Answer that question. Interviews are stressful enough without attempting to interpret or analyze what you think the reporter's motives might be. If you don't like the direction of a question, answer it briefly and bridge back to your own talking points.

Always try to use quotable quotes. Use colloquialisms, quote someone famous or use a memorable play on words, if appropriate, to make your point. Reporters love quotable quotes. They can make you look good in an interview and control the direction of the story.

Always back up message points with statistics and facts. When you use credible data to make your point in an interview, you earn respect and credibility.

Always remember that how you say it as important as what you say. In an interview, be genuine and sincere. Take some time before an interview to, as they say, get yourself in a good place. Go into an interview with a positive frame of mind. Don't be afraid to smile. Use your voice, eyes and expressions to show passion in your words.

Always maintain eye contact. Whether in a newspaper or television interview, look at the reporter and never allow your eyes to stray. Don't sneak a glance at the camera lens or someone standing nearby. Eye contact tells a reporter that this interview is the most important thing you are doing right now. If your eyes wonder during a television interview, the perception may be that you are nervous.

Always remember that a microphone is always "on." Never say anything silly or inappropriate assuming a microphone has been switched off. It can happen to anyone. Remember back in the 1980s when then-president Reagan, an old pro with the media who should have known better, jokingly said, "we start bombing Russia in five minutes?" A microphone was on and Reagan's playful remark made embarrassing headlines.

Always briefly summarize your key points at the end of the interview. You have the forum, the spotlight so make the most of it. A summary provides you with a final opportunity to deliver your three messages.

Now, for a short list of things to avoid doing in an interview:

Never talk off the record. It's a way to kill your credibility in working with the news media.

Never say anything you don't want to see in print or on the air. If you are angry at someone or a situation, don't use the interview as a forum to say something casually on the side that you didn't think a reporter will hear or use. An interview is not a time to kid around.

Never take it personally or get defensive. Reporters, in most cases, are just out doing their job of finding news stories. Work with them and everyone wins. The days of "ambush" journalism ended years ago.

Never assume an interview is a conversation. There is nothing casual or chatty about an interview, no matter how informal a particular reporter's style might be. A reporter is always working to find a good story.

Never make up answers. If you don't know, say so and that you will get the information and respond promptly.

So often when someone claims he or she has been misquoted in an interview, it's because of something the interviewee said. An apparent misquote usually happens because the person being interviewed has said something contradictory or ambiguous, even though the journalist usually and wrongfully gets the blame. It often happens by simply talking too much.

People who have mastered the discipline of being interviewed and talking with journalists on a high level of mutual respect and trust, know the effectiveness of using the news media as an enormously powerful and influential communication tool to reach vast and important audiences. Those are today's leaders.

The Benefits of Effective Media Relations

Media relations is all about communicating effectively to vast audiences through the news media.

An organization can't build credibility by purchasing a display advertisement on the front page of a major daily newspaper in America. Yet it is possible, through good media relations, for that organization to get a favorable news story on the front page, complete with the implied third-party credibility that comes from having a newspaper report good things about the organization. Effective media relations is the most powerful weapon in an organization's marketing arsenal.

Over the years, I have witnessed political greatness defined, such as the image of Ronald Reagan, through media relations, guided by people of intellect and media smarts, like my friend Michael Deaver.

My own work in media relations has centered on building corporate images and reputations in a competitive environment. Many times, I have worked with clients to devise ways to sell products through the powerful clout in the news media.

One of my favorite experiences happened in early 1990 when my client, London Records, asked me to find a way to propel sales of compact discs for the first Three Tenors Concert, which was about to happen in July of that year. London Records saw it as another opera recording, and that was a real challenge—opera recordings are not hot-selling items in America. The company's top executives had set a seemingly unattainable sales goal of 200,000 CDs during the first two months of the recording's release. It appeared to be an impossible task, since the previously biggest selling opera recording in America had sold a total of just 50,000 CDs over three years.

So off I flew to Rome to attend the concert and look for a story angle to drive sales. As I sat in the audience beside the legendary coloratura soprano Beverly Sills, watching the amazing performance by Luciano Pavarotti, José Carreras and Plácido Domingo, on a stage in the ancient Baths of Caracalla along the Appian Way in Rome, the idea struck me. This was not an opera performance but a historic event, a "never before" happening.

The royalty, celebrities and social elite of Europe had come together not for an opera concert but because they recognized history in the making. Pavarotti, Carreras and Domingo, all revered stars, had never performed together on the same stage, and it was making news around the world, except in the United States.

Once back home, I began making quiet soundings among friends and contacts in the national news media to find someone who might be interested in the story. The reaction was as if "opera" were a five-letter dirty word. No one had heard of the concert, and no one really cared. No one, except Cindy Carpien, the much-adored producer of National Public Radio's Weekend Edition on Saturday.

Cindy was intrigued by the fact that she hadn't heard of such a big event. There had been not one mention of it in the U.S. news media. Over a period of about a week, we talked several times to figure out how the story could be told on radio. It didn't seem feasible to interview only one of the tenors without the others. But to get all three together for such an interview would be impossible. So I proposed an interview with someone who had worked individually with each of the three tenors for 20 years and finally had the chance to work with all three together—the English recording engineer, James Locke. Cindy agreed.

James was a colorful interview. As excerpts from the first three tenors recording were played on NPR, he described the "magic" that filled the air that evening in Rome. Not once did he mention the word "opera" but instead described why the "historic event" had brought thousands of people together in Rome. The piece ran 12 minutes on a Saturday morning and was heard over nearly 400 NPR stations by an audience in the millions, primarily baby boomers, a generation that enjoys an appealing new trend.

Within a week, all 200,000 CDs of the first Three Tenors Concert recording were sold. It was the power of one cleverly developed story angle on a radio news program that was heard by the right audience. The recording went on to be the biggest-selling classical CD in history.

I wrote no news releases, no fact sheets, no media kits. The story happened by making phone calls to established contacts in the news media and working with them to develop an angle and provide someone to interview. As we've said elsewhere in this book, it's all about relationships and understanding how the media works.

Balanced and accurate news media coverage of a business or organization creates lasting goodwill, boosts an image, sells products and enhances credible influence more effectively than any other kind of mass communication. It will help to build a brand with enduring credibility.

Good media relations will help an organization break out of competitive clutter. It really doesn't matter whether you are the largest or number one. If the media likes you and is captivated by what you say, then you are perceived as a leader.

News in today's world is reported literally every minute, round-the-clock via the traditional channels of newspapers, wire services, magazines, television and radio but also through Internet Web sites and a variety of online sources, including blogs (Web journals).

But despite the diversity of today's types of media, media relations comes down to getting to know journalists and what they need to do their jobs, understanding what is news and what isn't, and working together with reporters on a professional level to provide the background information, facts and interviews they need to make a story happen.

And all along the way, those charged with media relations must be able to express enthusiasm without sounding like publicists. Clear and credible messages in everyday words must be crafted and neatly tucked inside the context of legitimate news. Savvy media relations techniques, consistently and professionally managed, will deliver impressive results. Great media coverage can be the stuff of legend.

# # #

0-595-34595-6

Printed in the United States
35019LVS00006B/391-465